P9-DFA-301

The
GARDEN
in
WINTER

The GARDEN in WINTER

PLANT FOR BEAUTY
AND INTEREST IN
THE QUIET SEASON

SUZY BALES

RODALE

Rodale books may be purchased for business or promotional use
or for special sales. For information, please write to:
Special Markets Department, Rodale Inc., 733 Third Avenue, New York, NY 10017

Printed in the United States of America
Rodale Inc. makes every effort to use acid-free ∞, recycled paper ♻.

Book design by Doug Turshen with David Huang
For photo credits, see page 196.

Library of Congress Cataloging-in-Publication Data

Bales, Suzanne Frutig.
    The garden in winter : plant for beauty and interest in the quiet season /
Suzy Bales.
        p.   cm.
    Includes bibliographical references and index.
    ISBN-13 978–1–59486–363–9 hardcover
    ISBN-10 1–59486–363–6 hardcover
    1. Winter gardening.   2. Plants in winter.   I. Title.
SB439.5B35   2007
635.9'53—dc22   200701875

Distributed to the trade by Holtzbrinck Publishers

2   4   6   8   10   9   7   5   3   1   hardcover

We inspire and enable people to improve their lives and the world around them
For more of our products visit **rodalestore.com** or call 800-848-4735

To Elvin McDonald and Barbara Winkler,
extraordinary editors and mentors

Contents

ix The Wonders
of a Winter Garden

1 Designing a Winter Garden

21 The Glory of Trees
and the Beauty of Bark

33 Colorful Conifers
and Broadleaf Evergreens

67 Deciduous Shrubs
That Dazzle

89 Perennial Pleasures:
Perennials and Grasses

111 Early-Blooming Bulbs

131 Winter Containers

153 Christmas from the Garden

190 Final Thoughts

SOURCES FOR WINTER PLANTS **192**   BIBLIOGRAPHY **194**
ACKNOWLEDGMENTS **195**   PHOTO CREDITS **196**   INDEX **197**

The Wonders of a Winter Garden

Although a lone flower blooming in a snowy bed gives my heart a jolt, it's the complementary combinations of plants that make a winter landscape endearing. Ironically, winter is when we need color the most but it is the season least planned and planted for color.

OPPOSITE: In the North, camellia blooms are often hit by snow and they don't take kindly to it like spring bulbs do.

a nd just for the record, T. S. Eliot got it wrong. January is the cruelest month—dark days amid bone-chilling cold. By April the delights of spring are galloping along. Then spring leapfrogs into summer. Summer cartwheels into fall. Fall, after a blaze of glory, collapses in a heap on home plate. Once fall fizzles out, the trees are denuded, the garden's bones are bare, and lost vistas are regained. Winter, the honest season, stands up naked, hiding nothing! Any plant left standing, bare or dressed, is an unsung hero.

I admire these adventurous plants routinely braving ice storms, blizzards, blankets of snow, high winds, gray days, and quickly plunging temperatures. It's hard not to when they bloom regardless of the weather.

Sensible shrubs wait until spring to bud. Cowards slumber. Gamblers set buds in the fall, clasp them tightly through winter gales, and plump them up for spring bloom. I love their optimism, each bud holding a promise of blooms.

When I planted our first gardens at our New York home in Oyster Bay on Long Island, I hadn't met many of these hardy fellows. I believed gardening was for warm weather. I gardened for flowers, and my borders overflowed three seasons of the year. Winter, I thought, was for napping. Over the decades, my eyes opened to the possibilities of winter flowers—hellebores, snowdrops, witch hazel, and the like, and I planted plenty. Once I looked beyond flowers, I planted a palette of evergreens, such as gold, green, and blue conifers, and variegated and boldly colored broadleaves much later.

I plan my winter garden to be colorful and engaging even on the darkest days. However, executing the plan is certainly *not* about laboring in the garden in wintertime—although when the weather is mild, I do enjoy being outdoors accomplishing something. Winter makes no demands on my time; it is only to be enjoyed, even if it is just looking out a window at a beautiful view. If I dig up a pot of snowdrops to bring inside or I prune the roses, it is what I feel like doing at the moment. Nothing needs to be done now. Everything can safely be put off until spring. Everything, that is, except keeping an eager eye on what is happening outdoors.

Winter is a fascinating season, a time to closely watch changes in plants. It is when I have seen miracles and been confounded by mysteries. Everything has a story to tell and secrets to reveal, from the design of a snowflake and the patterns of frost, to the first flowers piercing the cold ground, their blooms resting on a snowy pillow. The details fascinate me. Have you noticed that the first glimpse you have of hosta and peony noses piercing the ground in winter is red? When most bulbs first appear, their snouts are yellow. A touch of the sun is needed to jump-start photosynthesis to green them up. Virginia bluebells' first foliage appears black. Now why is that?

OPPOSITE: Bear's foot hellebore doesn't stop blooming or appear any worse for wear after a snowstorm. On many varieties each flower bract appears to be outlined in red lipstick.

A WALKABOUT

Walking around a garden after a snowstorm can be breathtakingly beautiful. Snow camouflages mistakes and refreshes the commonplace. Without snow, a winter landscape isn't as beautiful but there is more to discover. Walking around my garden in winter, I've learned more about what works and what doesn't than from any gardening book.

Returning to my garden on March 5, 2006, after a snowstorm trapped me on an airport runway for hours, I found so much to see. I stopped to admire snowdrops, winter aconite, crocus, hellebores, dwarf iris, compact Korean spice viburnum, witch hazel, and daffodils in bloom. I rubbed the buds of magnolia and willow, covered in silver fir, begging to be petted. The tree peony buds were in sharp contrast, plump and red. They hung on the bare limbs like silk tassels, frayed at the ends.

In the vegetable garden I discovered ruby chard shoots, small brightly colored foliage rising from the mushy remains of two of last summer's eight plants. That was a first! Self-seeded green leeks stood tall with only browned tips. They'll be baseballs of purple blooms by early summer. Egyptian onions too were green. I saw they had scooted farther afield from their original planting. Golden sage stood up, battered but brave. I was delighted—I often lose it after winter. The lavender was graying, all hint of blue gone, yet it released its perfume when I touched it. Ornamental kale no longer rested its head on the ground. It grew a foot over the winter and now had the figure of a palm tree, a tall, fat stem with a rounded top of mousy brown, crinkled foliage crowned with a cluster of still purple leaves.

In the rose garden, blue-gray catmint shoots were evident under the slate gray dried stems and foliage, ghosts of summer past. It was time to prune them.

The perennial border had turned the corner on winter and was silently slipping into spring. Sedum 'Autumn Joy', clary sage, and hollyhock showed new growth. Crocus and tulip sprouts were aboveground but not yet blooming. An empty pot on the nearby terrace had a wasp nest attached to its rim. I wondered if it had been there all summer hidden by the plant's foliage—how close had I been to being stung? Now was a good time to remove it.

Down by the pond, the early morning sun spread a golden glow among the grasses. The foot-high foliage of bearded iris was unscarred by winter's beating.

Strolling the woodland path, I glimpsed a tulip tree sporting a shawl of ivy high among its branches; another wore trousers woven of variegated euonymus. Farther along I was mesmerized by the intricate patterns of a lichen vest adorning an old oak. Once the trees leaf out, none of this is noticeable.

On a sloping path to the beach, blooms of winter aconite glowed among the

brambles. A solitary bloomer stood in the middle of the path. I never planted it there. Either the wind or the birds did.

Snow outlines the arching branches of the climbing rose, wheelbarrow, fence, and porch lattice, adding intricate patterns to the winter landscape.

The birds are probably the culprits that pecked the petals from a patch of woodland crocus. I've caught them doing it on the front lawn. But then, it might have been nibbling squirrels. They have been digging along my woodland path. I see them out my windows, but when the sneaky rodents hear me coming, they scurry away. The birds are more polite—they stay to chat when I approach.

On every walk around our property, more mysteries are revealed, and I have more questions than answers. How could a bird nest only 3 feet off the ground in the rose hedge escape the notice of our cat? Or did it? Why didn't the mother add its nest to the half-dozen others safely hidden in the ivy climbing the house? What prompted a few lilac buds to open several months early? How did the self-seeded nigella in the gravel driveway stay green all winter? Why wasn't it knocked down by the snow? Or was it and then it stood up again? Grasses do that! Why did the snapdragons survive one winter to bloom again but not another? Why do some plants blush in the cold air and others blacken? Why did the dwarf iris on one side of the garden bloom standing knee-high in snow, yet a few feet away, where the snow had melted, another clump slumbered, waiting a full week to make its appearance?

Every stroll I take around the garden is eye-opening. Sometimes I do it several times a day, each time noticing more. I always bundle up, although what I find in the garden warms me.

MOTHER NATURE'S MOODS

Winter is best known for Mother Nature's tantrums. They never cease to amaze me. She dances on the clouds and sends down billowing snow, points her icy finger at the newest blooms and stops them cold, and spins around, creating gusts of wind that swirl and wreak havoc as she dances.

Yet, after Mother Nature vents her wrath, the scene she leaves behind can be heart-stoppingly beautiful. Gusts of snow and ice form the most exquisitely beautiful patterns on Earth—the gleam of light passing through icicles, the miracle of a solitary bloom encased in ice. The sharp edges of frost highlight everything, a delicate fretwork against the blue sky. Each venture out is never the same.

All winter Mother Nature's hand hovers over a pause button. When she pushes it, everything freezes. When she lifts her finger, even for a day or two, bulbs push up and buds unfurl. The garden might sit for weeks at a time, then race along for a few days, only to be stopped by a cold spell. It is a time of false starts, interrupted growth spurts, and fragile beauty.

When a snowstorm passes, blue sky returns and the garden is blanketed in a snowy duvet, bejeweled with icy diamonds. How could you not love it? There is nothing as gorgeous and mesmerizing any other time of year. To be snowed in for a day or two, when everyone is safe, is a gift, an unplanned-for and most welcome vacation.

Yet, even as I write, many friends are preparing to skip winter entirely, moving south for several months, searching for the endless summer. They miss out on the perspective that winter brings. (I confess, though, that I never turn down an invitation for a week on a tropical island. But I could never skip winter entirely.) By March, I, too, need a break from winter's onslaught of cold gray weather. These are the dull days that need brightening, and in this book I write about many different approaches to accomplish that.

Use this book to cheer up your garden and enliven it with the plants and structures that are comforting in winter. It is the golden garden circle—you cheer up your garden and it cheers you. A winter garden is about possibilities, the relationship you develop with Mother Nature, and the secrets she reveals to you about your garden.

The simplest way to break up a monotonous landscape is by adding structures, garden ornaments, winter containers, and a broad range of colorful plants, including early blooms and berries that cling to tree and shrub branches through the winter. Interesting seed heads should be left intact. Not only do they feed the birds (the birds are certainly welcome as they entertain us with their antics and songs), but on some plants, such as grasses, their dead stems protect their crowns from the elements. Conifers, often the last planted, are the first to give winter pleasure. They look much the same year-round.

Color in any form—structures, conifers, bark, berries, and foliage—brighten up a drab day. Green in winter is to the garden what meat and potatoes are to the body: comfort food. Brighter colors—blue, red, and gold—are much more exciting, like sugary desserts, but best used in small amounts. Winter bloomers trigger spontaneous smiles.

All winter Mother Nature's hand hovers over a pause button.

It takes time to get to know a piece of ground and what works where. Every garden is a collaboration between three strong-willed partners—the gardener, the plants, and Mother Nature. Each is determined to have its own way. Moving slowly is often better in garden design. An instant garden doesn't always sit right. Anyone whose garden looks exactly as it was first planted probably doesn't have a very interesting garden. There are always plants that need to be shuffled around before they are properly partnered and settled in. So take your time.

Learn what works and what doesn't by doing. A little bit of a devil-may-care attitude is necessary in every good garden, but especially in a winter garden. Every planting is a gamble, with the odds mostly in our favor. So place a few five- or ten-dollar bets with Mother Nature and don't be a sore loser if they don't work out. It's satisfying and rewarding to create your own refuge. And don't hesitate to ask directions all along the way.

The plants I mention in this book are by no means inclusive. There are more plants that perform daring feats in winter than I was able to squeeze in. Some, such as hellebores and witch hazels, could fill a book by themselves.

Get Your Dates Straight

Never trust a calendar! Mine claims that winter lasts for 3 months all across the country. It pays no attention to the weather. Winters vary!

Freezing temperatures with snow, sleet, and ice, define winter for me where I live in New York. Winters in Atlanta are considerably shorter than those in Maine. A daffodil that blooms in Atlanta in January won't awaken in Maine until late April or May.

My winter ends with the first full, all-out, no-holds-barred bloom of scilla covering my hillside and species tulips cavorting with early daffodils. They are the harbingers of spring and they never lie. Even if a late snowstorm brazenly contradicts them, it realizes its mistake and leaves in a hurry.

Winter is unpredictable. Even plants that reliably return don't keep the same schedule from year to year. The date of their arrival may differ in weeks or even months from one year to another. In my journal, I noted snowdrop clumps that every year bloomed in late December didn't appear until March in another. This year 'February Gold' daffodils bloomed in late February instead of March, the only time in the 25 years since I planted them. Strangely, the snowdrops were barely aboveground and not blooming, stalled that way for weeks. While the typical lineup in the parade of bloom stays pretty much the same—snowdrops, winter aconite, witch hazel, hellebores, crocus, scilla, dwarf iris, puschkinia,

and so on—their first appearance, length of stay, and departure time are unpredictable. In a slow, drawn-out winter, each has its own time to be admired; in a fast winter, overlapping bloom causes a sensation.

Unpredictable things happen in a winter garden—one reason it holds my attention. I never know what's going to happen next. One winter is not like another. In winter more than in other seasons, meteorological extremes seem to be the norm. The truth is our weather is very rarely normal. The average snowfall in my area for January is 8.6 inches, but in 2005 we were buried in 29 inches and in 2006 we were dusted with only 4 inches. February averages 9.3 inches, but in 2005 we topped out at 20 inches and in 2006, 14 inches. Temperatures varied, too. It is not unusual to have 60°F one day and below zero the next. As the weather changes dramatically, so does the garden. There are usually a few casualties. But I've learned not to be too quick to say goodbye. I never count the dead until May. All too often I've discovered that the plant was merely playing dead, that there was still life in its roots. The good news is that amid winter's murder and mayhem, death and destruction, miracles, beauty, and rebirth reign supreme.

OPPOSITE: Snowdrops have the amazing ability to grow and bloom even when surrounded by snow. They are traditionally the first winter bulbs to bloom.

HOW TO USE THIS BOOK

Summer polishes the glow in us all. But in winter most of us become dried, frosted, and lethargic. I know I do. So I wrote this book to highlight winter's possibilities. I hope to wake up your senses so you'll smell the witch hazel, pet the yaks, and enjoy choruses of snowdrops and scilla. Hopefully I will arouse your curiosity and you will want to take a closer look at what happens outside your back door. Winter's plants are an example for us all.

The first chapter, "Designing a Winter Garden," is an overview of how to design winter features in a garden. It is also a place to check off what you already have and to see how you might supplement what is there.

The next five chapters introduce the plants and their features: trees, bark, conifers, evergreens, perennials, grasses, and bulbs that add color and interest to brighten winter's gray landscape. Plants from each of these chapters are necessary to make a pleasing garden. Even if you only plant one winter-blooming shrub in spring and a bucketful of bulbs in fall, you will find you enjoy your winter landscape so much more. Once you start, planting a few things each spring and fall to pep up your winter views could become a habit.

This is not an exhaustive list of the plants available for winter pleasures, but rather the ones that are the easiest to grow and the most readily available. It is a good place to start. Each zone has its top performers. Your county extension office or your local nursery can give you a list appropriate for your own area.

Winter won't seem as empty if all-weather containers as described in "Winter Containers" are planted with conifers or stuffed with assorted greens to decorate an entrance or enliven a view.

In the last chapter, I write about Christmas—my favorite holiday—from the garden. I take pleasure in bringing the garden indoors at this time of year. When the house is decorated and fragrant with greens, it is the warmest and coziest time of the year and the best way to celebrate the changing seasons.

Throughout the book are sidebars filled with interesting facts about everything from the intricacies of snowflakes to drying flowers to "fire in ice" sculptures. I hope that in this book you will find the seeds of inspiration to make your own winter wonderland.

OPPOSITE: Every detail in the seed head of sweet autumn clematis is highlighted by the snow.
BELOW: Upside-down icicles planted in the snow around a pillar candle bring the outside in and add sparkle to holiday festivities.

Designing a Winter Garden

On snowy mornings as I look out from my bedroom window, the beauty of the winter garden always takes me by surprise. The palette is a chiaroscuro of black, white, and gray—a glorious pen and ink drawing. I notice how the ice crystals play up the outlines of the vegetable garden and

OPPOSITE: A cover of snow brings out the bones of the garden. The espaliered fence of fruit trees, arbor, front lawn, shrubs, and trees are all revealed as if they were in a pen and ink drawing.

1

The boxwood hedges, stone wall, and bare branches of trees give structure and a frame to the garden that is arresting year-round.

how shapes are minimized to basic forms, stark and oddly arresting. The muted shadings of the conifers—blue, gold, silver, bronze—stand out against the blanket of white and the textures of the grasses are so distinct that I could almost touch them. Again and again I appreciate the subtlety of the treasures in my winter landscape, and I always vow to make it even better the following year.

A TIME TO PAUSE, A TIME TO STUDY

Winter-weary souls, take heart. This is the perfect season to study your garden, appreciate its bounty, learn its limitations, and plan its future. Jot down what you like and what you're missing. Note changes to make in spring. Start with the plantings near the house, along the driveway, and along the entry walk. Look too at the views from the windows. What would you like to see from your window when you first awake? Is there a focal point? Does the view hold your interest?

To help you along, take some pictures. I use a digital camera and snapshots of the same sites through the seasons. Sometimes I print out the pictures and roughly sketch shapes on them to see how a tree or a shrub might alter the perspective. Other times, so much jumps out in the photo that the answer is obvious. But one thing is certain: Taking pictures so I can look back is the quickest way for me to move forward.

Taking pictures so I can look back is the

THE SIGNIFICANCE
OF STRUCTURE

Winter reveals the framework of the garden. As shrubs and trees drop their leaves and flowers bite the dust, strong forms and patterns stand out. Some are man-made, like fences, arbors, arches, paths, and even raised beds. Others are Mother Nature's gifts: stately conifers, sculptural trees, rounded shrubs. They break up the bleak landscape and give the eye a place to focus.

Man-made structures abound in nurseries, home centers, and mail order catalogs, and while they need less nurturing than plants, they can be equally difficult to choose. Twig bowers, copper triptychs, lattice screens, iron obelisks—how do you pick? To my mind, you need to take the cue from the style of your house. If you live in a classic colonial, structures should be tailored, timeless, and formal rather than fanciful. This is the place for a cedar arbor or wrought iron tuteur. A house that's more cottage-y calls for pickets, lattice, and rustic pieces like willow arches and twiggy trellises. A Victorian home demands something more elaborate—arbors and fences with fantastic finials and complicated curlicues. Contemporary houses can go classic or cutting edge with copper arches, galvanized metal pillars, or whorled trellises that act as sculptures for vines to climb. That said, you should follow your own personal taste. What's most important is to choose items for vertical impact.

Even though such structures provide year-round interest, it's fun to gussy them up for winter when their plant coverings have died back. String bare garden tepees with white mini lights. Place a decorated Christmas tree in a gazebo. Hang tiny birdhouses from a lattice screen. Or borrow this idea from my friend and expert gardener, Elvin McDonald. Not content to let the lath trellises on his garage stand naked, he suspends solid colored glass ornaments in the openings. His birdbath is piled high with a pyramid of silver Christmas balls with one gold one set on top (see page 181). Christmas lights, he notes, are great at night but the balls gleam and sparkle all day for a new take on garden "bling."

Garden ornaments also offer form and structure. A birdbath, for instance, steps forward in a drab landscape, calling attention to its shape and placement. The same goes for a stone bench, a cement statue, a zinc-topped sundial. Any of these help define depth and distance, which are sorely needed in winter.

quickest way for me to move forward.

Tony and Mary Smith's garden on Long Island, in New York, was designed to be beautiful all four seasons. The red branches of the coral bark maple and the golden yucca add bright color to the somber scene. The serpentine stem of wisteria climbing the arbor is a natural sculpture. Conifers and deciduous shrubs add a variety of shapes and the decorative fence along one side sets boundaries without enclosing the garden. Put all the pieces together and there is a lot to enjoy in the winter landscape.

Mother Nature's Architecture

Trees, shrubs, and evergreen vines are living sculptures. They draw the eye up or down, block a view, and produce focal points. Unlike man-made structures, these grow up and out. Keep in mind the mature size of the items you buy and consider which take well to pruning and which don't. Since I go into the particulars of specific plants in the following chapters, I won't detail their attributes here, but I do want to make a few general points.

Hedges are one of the best ways to give a garden pattern, structure, and privacy. They can be evergreen or deciduous, tall or short, berried or not. Low ones of boxwood or yew can act as borders for other plantings. Taller versions act as walls to enclose a space entirely or to block a view. We have a 10-foot-long, 5-foot-high **'Princess' holly hedge** that separates our side terrace from the cars that pull up to the house. It gives us privacy year-round and I wouldn't trade it for anything. More 'Princess' holly backs the rose garden in a graceful semicircle, while a border of **boxwood** fronts it. More boxwood rims a nearby fountain lending its warm green to the cold, gray cement. These three hedges play an important role all year but are especially beautiful in winter when the flowers have disappeared. They add depth and dimension to what would otherwise be a flat, boring expanse.

CAPTURING FRAGRANCE

I mentioned that hedges are the architectural walls of a garden, but I didn't elaborate on how these walls can help create a perfumed paradise. An outdoor space, enclosed by hedges, is shielded from the wind. The heat of the sun is trapped within and builds up during the day so it remains warm later into the night. This means that the vapors of a flower's aroma will be held, then released ever so slowly, rather than dispersing with the slightest breeze.

Even stopping the wind on only the prevailing side makes a difference. A semicircle of 'Princess' holly, a row of evergreens, or a fence festooned with an evergreen vine all help stay the wind and capture the perfume of plants. But if you have the space, there is nothing more magical on a frosty day than a "room," bordered by hedges or walls and planted with fragrant, early blooming bulbs and shrubs. My choices for such a plot would be snowdrops, winter aconite, scented daffodils, snow crocus, and witch hazels. All can make themselves known by their scents alone.

Besides holly and boxwood, good hedging choices are **yew, privet,** and **euonymus.** Or choose conifers with a columnar form, such as a statuesque arborvitae, perhaps, or a tall skinny juniper. Better yet, weave a tapestry of different greens and golds. At Powell Gardens, in Kansas City, Missouri, a trio of conifers alternating in a different order forms a hedge down the middle of a perennial border. The conifers have similar growth rates and shapes so it works. The trio includes blue redcedar (*Juniperus virginiana* 'Glauca'), emerald sentinel redcedar (*Juniperus virginiana* 'Emerald Sentinel'), and Berckman's golden oriental arborvitae (*Thuja orientalis* 'Aurea Nana').

It is a wonderful backdrop for the flowers three seasons of the year and the main attraction in winter.

A hedge can be more interesting sitting in a contrasting groundcover. A semicircle of **inkberry** resting in a bed of ivy screens a seating area by our pond, hiding it from view of the house. This green oasis knows no season. It is evergreen and restful year-round.

Another hedged-in haven is my own secret garden, complete with a bench and hammock, nestled behind a grouping of deciduous shrubs, trees, and evergreens. It's all but invisible in summer, but in winter when the shrubs have dropped their foliage, it is a peekaboo garden that allows just a glimpse of the early spring bulbs within.

Like hedges, trees and shrubs can also form a framework. They'll establish an airier outline but still will accomplish the feat of defining a space. Even without leaves, my row of espaliered apple and pear trees draws a definite line for the eye to follow; the same goes for a series of forsythia bushes or an alley of London plane trees.

While many of us think of conifers as the ideal winter trees, deciduous trees are worth considering for their striking naked silhouettes. Apple trees come to mind immediately; their gnarled trunks and branches twist and turn like a Giacometti statue—such beautiful bones are meant to be displayed. Even a single specimen of Japanese maple is stunning against a dark gray sky. Smallish trees also look splendid grouped together or placed in the center of parterres. Consider also positioning trees and shrubs in containers and using them to anchor a border or lend vertical interest to a series of parterres. The pots lend more heft and stature and really draw the eye.

Massive hedges clipped in geometric shapes have the same visual weight as boulders in the landscape. They are mesmerizing in a winter landscape.

Hedges are one of the best ways to give a garden pattern, structure, and privacy.

WALLS WITH GARDEN PICTURES

Another way to add intriguing pattern to the garden is with vines. **Climbing hydrangea,** for example, creates a marvelous motif along a wall with its reddish brown stems. It clings by sending out aerial rootlets, thin as yarn, that grab onto brick, stone, or wood. Call me lazy, but I never deadhead the spring flowers; they dry beautifully intact and cling through the year, adding another layer of beauty to a lush embroidery that lasts all winter long.

Other deciduous vines deliver a similar benefit. Many roses have bright red or light green new stems that contrast nicely with their gray trunks. The tracery of canes is striking on our stucco walls and the few rose hips that cling add sparkling dots of color.

Evergreen vines such as **ivy, cross vine (*Bignonia capreolata*),** or **winter jasmine (*Jasminum nudiflorum*)** lend both pattern and color to a drab surface. On the stucco pillars at our entrance, several different evergreen variegated ivies and cross vine tangle together into a wonderful tapestry. On top of them, long and leggy rose stems swag and cross to add another dimension. They are all compatible aboveground because their roots are planted 6 feet apart belowground. It is a happy combination that changes with the seasons.

PLANTING PARTNERS

I find that planting in pairs of colors is a simple way to come up with pleasing design combinations, and bulbs accomplish this quite well. They can be partnered with a flowering shrub, a conifer, a groundcover, or another bulb that blooms at the same time for an interesting effect.

At our house, the first shrubs to bloom in the new year are the **witch hazels** clustered in an island planting at a curve in our driveway. *Hamamelis* × *intermedia* 'Diane' flaunts her burnt orange tassels in mid-January, followed closely by the sunny yellow crimpled petals of 'Arnold's Promise'. Early daffodils at their feet end the winter display. Although they rarely bloom together, the succession of blossoms always catches my attention. However, to start the show even sooner, I'm going to layer Siberian squill above the daffs next fall. This way the witch hazel will start the season swimming in a pool of blue, then when the daffs flower, the shrubs will be walking on sunshine.

Forsythia too takes on new glamour where I've surrounded it with the glow of daffodils. The double dose of yellow is a knockout. Yellow flowers are also fabulous coupled with blue, a pairing that is justly famous. The golden blossoms of **winter jasmine (*J. nudiflorum*)** seem more lustrous with glory-of-the-snow and scilla at its feet, while *Salix discolor*, a silver-gray **pussy willow**, easily settles in among the blues and yellows of glory-of-the-snow, scilla, winter aconite, and daffodils. For some reason, this combo of colors makes the silver glisten more intensely and the silver heightens the tints of the bulbs.

OPPOSITE: Climbing hydrangea with its lacy dried flowers decorates our arbor even in winter. The white flowers bloom in late spring then dry to a warm honey tone. Through the arch, a bit of 'Goldheart' ivy can be seen climbing the carpentry shop.

Across the front lawn, **red-twig dogwood (*Cornus alba*)** is teamed with assorted bulbs, from snowdrops through daffodils and species tulips, since the dogwood's bright red bark sets the garden aflame until late April. Another bulb grouping—snowdrops, crocus, scilla, and daffodils—crowd the base of my star magnolia. Although this tree really blooms in early spring, I mention it here since we're usually still being buffeted by high winds and snowstorms. The succession of bulbs makes it seem as if the tree blooms longer, when in reality the flowers last little more than a week.

The February **daphne (*Daphne mezereum*)** is at the shady end of my flower border. It has white flowers that appreciate a touch of blue from a skirt of **glory-of-the-snow (*Chionodoxa*)**. Likewise, **cotoneaster (*Cotoneaster horizontalis*)**, with its burgundy foliage and red berries, looks fully dressed with red species tulips coming up through its branches.

The simplest planting is to gussy up your grass with a patchwork of blooms.

Drooping leucothoe (*Leucothoe fontanesiana*) wears many different coats, from a solid burgundy to one speckled with red and white on a green background. The burgundy cultivars shine when paired with white or yellow daffs and 'Rainbow', which is splotched with pink, cream, green, and copper, is right at home with red species tulips.

Evergreen groundcovers—grass, pachysandra, vinca, ajuga, ivy, creeping euonymus (to name just some)—provide dramatic backdrops for flowering bulbs or even red- or yellow-twigged plants. The groundcover insulates the bulbs from quick freezes and thaws, keeps mud from splattering on them, and hides their unsightly exits. If the groundcover flowers at the same time the bulbs are blooming, as in vinca and daffodils for instance, you've hit the jackpot.

The simplest planting is to gussy up your grass with a patchwork of blooms. The early risers—snowdrops, crocus, scilla, and glory-of-the snow—die back before the lawn needs mowing. To accomplish this without any damage, just slice the top layer of lawn, pull it back and tuck a dozen bulbs underneath, and tap the lawn back down in place. Taller bulbs—daffodils and species tulips—dance above groundcovers that don't need mowing. Plant these in individual holes or dig a hole the size of a dinner plate and plop in six to eight. In most cases, the groundcover will quickly grow back to cover the planting.

PASS THE BLAME!

When things don't go well for me, I blame the soil, the weather, or Wall Street—it really doesn't matter which. What's important is that a gardener passes the blame along regularly. If you don't, it is easy to get caught up in the brown thumb syndrome and believe you can't garden well. A bad attitude has killed more potential gardens than any other cause. All gardening is trial and error, all sites have their own quirks, and even the best designers experience some failures in every garden they plant. There are just too many variables and unknowns when you work with living things. A garden has to evolve. That is what makes it a lively sport, full of surprises, both good and bad.

Armchair Indulgences

There are few things better than curling up in front of a blazing fire with a stack of garden catalogs to begin planning next year's gardens. For now, wrapped in a brown fleece bathrobe, I am, not unlike a hibernating grizzly, content. In the face of the warmth of the fire, my desire for activity has gone up in smoke. Instead, while I am in my armchair, my imagination can run wild with possibilities without a touch of practicality. In my relaxed and dreamy state, I am very susceptible to the fiction of the stack of catalogs on my lap.

Garden catalogs foster wonderful fantasies. Some are also highly entertaining. The newest plant introductions can be found here as well as unique and unusual plants. And good catalogs are a useful addition to a garden library—many are filled with sound advice—and they can be carried into the yard as a resource. If they land in the mud, most likely a new one is in the mail.

Is it necessary to forewarn you that a catalog's whole purpose in life is to present plants as irresistible? I take no responsibility for excessive ordering or for plants bought without a thought of where to plant them. I am a plant addict, and while my habit improves my life, it also takes a toll on my pocketbook. The more catalogs I read, the more new plants I meet; the more plants I meet, the more I want; the more I want, the more I buy—and every one I buy, I have to plant.

Each winter I try to restrain myself so I don't get swept into the depths of my pocketbook. I circle every plant I want on one day, then check it another day to be sure I really "need" it. The problem is, I usually do.

The *David Austin Handbook of Roses* gets my heart rate up, simply sitting in a chair. One can never have too many roses, especially climbers. As I look out my windows, I envision more roses tumbling over the fence, soaring upward against a bare wall, and wreathing the garage window. I'm even tempted to plant a climber up my neighbor's garden shed.

Song Sparrow includes a great assortment of perennials and shrubs, I make a beeline for the peonies. I've never seen the range of colors, shapes, and bloom times anywhere else. By ordering early, mid, and late bloomers, I have more than 6 weeks of peonies.

Brent and Becky's Bulbs is one of the reasons I always plant bulbs in spring and fall. They are always expanding the possibilities of my garden by introducing new bulbs and noting the ones that are critter-proof. I find that I always have room for another one.

The *White Flower Farm* catalog is garden poetry and a top source for readable prose and information. There is always something to learn while perusing it and something new I can't live without.

I have touched on a few of my favorites, but there are hundreds of specialty catalogs not as well-known but equally valuable. Order catalogs now as a vaccine against a potential epidemic of cabin fever in January.

Anyone with limited space should be forewarned—you may drown in a pool of indecision.

AN INVITATION OUT

If your garden is a destination and a place you walk in all kinds of weather, then plant winter combinations that give you reason to go into it. Add excitement with a cameo grouping, such as the combination of an early-blooming shrub with bulbs that flower at the same time, which will appear suddenly as you round a corner.

However, I caution you, too. I lined an out-of-the-way path with assorted primroses that bloomed successively over a 3-month period. To reach it, I had to walk down the main woodland path, veer to the left at the bottom, round a corner, and walk uphill. I missed most of the primrose splendor because this just wasn't a route I took each day. If the weather was dreary, it didn't occur to me to visit. Over the following years, I divided the primroses and planted them elsewhere—around a tree on the front lawn, edging a bed in the back, beneath shrubs around the house. Now I can spy them from various windows and walk by some almost daily. How else would I know that a renegade yellow hose-in-hose primrose beauty was nestled under its foliage on January 2?

A garden needs continual editing. It is necessary to regularly remove and add plants, even discard nonperformers, refining what you see. Watch and learn from the plants and their behavior. Notice what blooms at the same time and perhaps move them together. I hope this chapter will get you started. I have listed some wonderful books in the bibliography (page 194) that could help, such as *Wonders of the Winter Landscape*, by Vincent A. Simeone, and *Winter Ornamentals*, by Daniel Hinkley, but the best ideas will come to you from your garden itself.

OPPOSITE: When the redbud blooms, the daffodils, snowflakes, hellebores, and first hybrid tulips dance at its feet to announce spring is marching in.

DESIGN DO'S AND DON'TS

DO keep an eye on other gardens, both public and private, for ideas about plant combinations, layout, and structure. When you discover something you want to try, sketch it out or jot it down in a notebook. What you are really doing is forcing yourself to look closer at how gardens are constructed, and your observations will result in a better design at home.

DO sketch out the outlines of beds and borders with a garden hose. The hose's flexibility makes it easy to change the shape as you change your mind. While you're at it, play with different forms, from semicircles to ovals to free-form designs.

DO use plants to light up the garden. Play with variegated shrubs and gold and silver conifers to brighten a dreary winter day. Grasses, too, add a layer of light, since many of them fade to blonde.

DON'T plant trees and shrubs immediately. Let them remain in their pots or balls of burlap, positioned where you think they should go, and wait a few days. Observe them from different viewpoints, see how they work with the traffic flow, and then decide. This way when you do plant them there will be no surprises—except perhaps one. They always look smaller when lowered into the ground.

DON'T forget the view from windows; it's just as important as a walk-around perspective. Plan attractive vignettes you can spot from windows and you'll be on your way to a prettier landscape.

DON'T be afraid to move plants around as your garden evolves. Playing shuffleboard with plants is a favorite pastime of experienced gardeners. Remember, not everyone gets everything right the first time, not even the experts.

Dashing Through the Garden

Standing on your head in Robert Dash's garden might help you see how he created it. Then again, maybe not! For 40 years he has been challenging the way gardens are planted, paved, pruned, and painted.

In 1966, Dash, a prominent artist with paintings in more than two dozen museums, including Boston's Museum of Fine Arts and New York's Guggenheim, purchased an old barn and several sheds on 1.9 acres in the Hamptons on Long Island. He named it Madoo, "my dove" in Gaelic. Ever since, he has moved back and forth between his paintbrush and his garden trowel; as he explains, "I bore easily."

All this movement caused his paint to spill over into his garden. Forget respectable neutral colors; think chartreuse, Chinese red, mustard, yellow, blue, mauve, and lavender. Bold paint colors that sting indoors, sing outdoors. A pair of gateposts, a gazebo, the doors to the shed and two houses, an outside staircase, and an Oriental bridge explode in painted colorful bursts.

This is a sure way to bring more color to a winter landscape.

Dash believes like Monet before him that mauve is the very color of the air. "White," he declares, "is too blinding outdoors." Black is used to make something disappear.

Breezes from the beach bring a lot of salt that wears away the paint. So he repaints the colorful structures every 2 years, occasionally changing their colors.

The garden is divided into rooms, each designed like a composition on a canvas, infused with color and imagination. The rooms are connected by paths and, as Dash explains, are designed "to deliberately guide the visitor into loitering with good intent." However, if a plant invades a path, and it looks right, the plant wins: Dash moves the path. Plants come first, structures second.

Plants can't do exactly as they like, however. Dash corrects their behavior with pruning year-round. "Pruning" he says, "can make new the old. It's like a haircut." In winter he prunes for sculptural heft and general shape. In summer he prunes to let the light in. Pruning reveals the architecture of the plant and exposes the bark for winter interest. Pruning the bottom branches of a shrub removes the growth that dies as it ages, speeding up growth in the higher branches.

When a grove of black pines was decimated by blue spore disease, Dash replaced it with a grove of ginkgo. He knew they would survive because the poet Frank O'Hara said that they were as old as cockroaches. But they looked lonely, so he added boxwood pruned into balls to make a composition. He calls it "a riff on Alice and her game of croquet."

Rhododendron, magnolia, and cedar create a bank along one side of the grove and are limbed up to allow more light to reach a golden euonymus. Dash says the bank "gives the composition an almost arena-like enclosure, all of which can be viewed from a stool in the double-roofed gazebo."

Privet is the signature plant of the Hamptons for screening out the prying eyes of neighbors, but Dash bucked tradition and pruned out their lower lateral growth. His privet appear as small trees "with legs like ballerinas" dancing in a flowering groundcover. The pruned-up hedge still marks the garden's boundaries with spring blossoms overhead but now has good airflow below.

Madoo is Robert Dash's private home, but since 1994 he has opened it to the public a few days a week. For more information, contact the Madoo Conservancy, 618 Sagg Main Street, PO Box 362, Sagaponack, New York 11962, or look online at www.madoo.org.

Robert Dash's grove of ginkgo trees underplanted with boxwood balls symbolizes Alice in Wonderland's game of croquet. Even in February without snow, it is an arresting composition.

GARDEN ORNAMENTS

A whimsical way to lighten up the gloom of winter is to carefully place garden ornaments in strategic spots. I'm not talking about garden gnomes and flamingos, although I admit they can be funny. And a snowy cap on a half-naked cherub is also more amusing than trite.

I prefer to consider what would naturally be in my garden and then play with that image. For example, in our woods mushrooms grow wild, so a pair of oversize ones look right at home. Rusty iron acorns are portable and embellish a winter bloomer or sit quietly at the base of a winter container. Birdhouses count as ornaments, too, especially if they are colorful.

On one side of our pond, I've placed a rusty heron with a fish in its mouth. It reminds me of the heron that walked up from the pond and into the open door of our dining room. (I'm not sure who was more surprised, the heron or I.) On the other side is a pelican. I admit it belongs in the South, but it was a gift. If you like the giver, you tend to cherish the gift.

At our house, iron and stone rabbits mingle with the real thing. Last March we found a nest of three bunnies under the foliage of grape hyacinth in our new winter garden. I assume their mother chose the spot because the digging was easy, but it's a hard place to go unnoticed. Between my dog, the foxes, and the raccoons, they'll have to struggle. I wish them well and will happily share the treats in our vegetable garden with them come summer. I love catching a glimpse of them hopping away.

Antique English saddle stones, once used to hold up a corncrib so the critters couldn't get in, look like giant mushrooms in our woods. OPPOSITE: A wire topiary rabbit covered in moss and sprouting ivy is a whimsical addition to our garden in every season.

Frost

Frost is mischievous, wreaking havoc in the garden when it arrives unexpectedly, like an assassin in the night. Then again, it can stop me in my tracks when I see its breathtakingly beautiful frostwork, like spun sugar, coating the pattern that moisture forms when it is frozen on a windowpane.

Surprisingly, 75 percent of the world's landmass is visited by frost, the icy crystals that cover a cold surface. Frost can be devastating and cruel, arriving too early or extremely late when it's not expected. If it hits the South where it rarely visits, it can cause the costly ruin of a Florida orange crop.

Frost forms faster on colder surfaces. The composition of the object and how well it absorbs sunlight affects whether it will be frosted, too. A lawn and a car, for example, absorb less sunlight than a driveway or a wooden deck. Often I see frost on the car and the lawn but not on the warmer pavement.

If frost stays for a few hours on a tender plant, the moisture in the plant's foliage freezes and ruptures its cell membranes. Once plants are frostbitten, they are injured; susceptible ones blacken and some die. Becoming aware of the different types of frost—hoarfrost, black frost, white frost, glazed frost, ground frost, air frost— shows how complicated understanding frost can be.

Frost can be harmless if its visit is brief. After a light frost, many annuals bloom again as if nothing has happened. Unfortunately, too many gardeners pull up their annuals in early fall, leaving big blanks in their garden. If they had just tidied them up and let them be, they might have a month or more of bloom. Occasionally, some annuals surprise me— snapdragons and salvia, for example—by living through a Zone 7 winter to bloom again.

Frost heaving, an upthrust of the ground caused by freezing that expands moist soil, tossing up newly planted perennials and bulbs, can be a killer. If left out of the ground for a few days, new plants can dry up and die. Consequently, it is important to walk around after the first heavy frost and check on your "babies." You might have to tuck them back in. If you do, they'll be fine. Established plants and bulbs have deeper roots to anchor them, so they are not as susceptible to quick freezing and thawing temperatures.

Zone maps measure temperatures, giving a rough estimate of fluctuations in your climate. Knowing your first frost date in the fall and last frost recorded in the spring lets you know when it is safe to plant and when to harvest. It makes you a better gardener, keeping you on the lookout for Jack Frost's visits.

Keeping your own records helps even more. Every garden has microclimates, areas that are warmer or colder than what is normal for your area. A simple way to find them is to plant the same early bulbs in different places in your garden. They won't all bloom at the same time. Peak bloom from one area to another only yards away could be days or even weeks apart. Once you discover the warmest areas in your garden, you can plant marginally hardy plants there.

Les Brake (see page 140) had so many plants

come through the first few winters he spent in Alaska, he thought he was gardening in England. It was the 6-foot snow cover that protected his perennials and kept the ground from deep freezes. Snow insulates the ground. Les wrote, "Despite 30 to 40 nights below zero, with 129 inches of snow cover, even lamb's ears come through green. That's the power of snow."

Then Les experienced a "blue screamer," a winter with no snow cover until February. The ground froze to a depth of 10 feet and he lost 2,000 of his 2,100 bulbs and most of his perennials. The survivors, "winter-proof perennials," were almost all from high altitudes—Himalayan blue poppies, Siberian iris, delphiniums, and alpine

primroses. They are now his garden's staples. That winter taught him a number of lessons—allow magically hardy perennials to set and drop seed in case the mother plant dies, and grow more alpine plants. Some of his annuals drop so much seed that they return more reliably than the perennials. These are what he calls his "annual perennials."

But don't forget, frost is necessary for many of the plants we grow in the North to bloom. Without frost or prolonged cold, bulbs and lilacs won't flower. If I wanted a tropical garden, I'd move south.

In early March with the first daffodils in bloom, frost outlines the trees and shrubs, adding a sparkle to the woodland walk.

The Glory of Trees and the Beauty of Bark

A wise man, when asked what he would do if he knew it was the last day of his life, replied, "Plant a tree." And I must say I agree. Looking out the window on a bitterly cold day, I marvel at the 130-year-old pin oaks lining our driveway. Their sturdy trunks bear

OPPOSITE: The Adirondack wilderness is an interesting place to hike even in winter. The beech tree holds its leaves all winter until the new ones emerge. It looks like a ghost of summer past. The shiny trunk of the yellow birch glows in the sun and the conifers add a colorful contrast.

up to winter winds with bold bravado, and their bare branches create intricate patterns against the darkening clouds. These specimens are so strong and stalwart, they actually seem to be holding up the sky. Smaller trees might not have the same majesty, but they too connect the earth to the sky and provide shape and texture that is greatly appreciated during this often bleak season. I think, for instance, of a weeping cherry: The delicate fretwork of its bending branches forms a stunning silhouette. Or a crab apple, denuded of its leaves, offers the gift of bright red berries. So, when choosing trees, I now select some specifically for winter interest, which usually means they are glorious in other seasons as well.

LIVING SCULPTURES

Long after flowers have faded and leaves have fallen, the landscape metamorphoses into a sculpture garden, with trees as the major attraction. To be sure, evergreens and conifers produce a rich backdrop, but it is the deciduous trees that stand out like beautifully crafted pieces of art. Weeping, spreading, conical, columnar, pyramidal, round, or vaselike, there is a shape for every site. Here are some of my choices for winter impact.

On my winter cross-country-ski outings in the forests of the Adirondacks, the **American beech (*Fagus grandifolia*)** always makes me smile. It is a ghost of summer past with its dried khaki leaves hanging on through torrents of terrible weather. Sure, some leaves blow off, but the miracle is that so many cling. The trees look fully clothed. And when the sun hits them, the foliage glows like polished copper. The tree's classic round shape and smooth gray bark complete the picture. Often I stumble upon a thicket of beech, with one larger tree ringed by upstarts. (I'm not that good of a skier.) It freely sends out suckers, which could be a problem in a small garden.

The **European weeping beech (*F. sylvatica* 'Pendula')** is interesting for other reasons. It completely drops its drawers, shedding all its leaves and revealing gnarly branches, bent and twisted—mesmerizing to be sure.

Most trees with a so-called weeping habit simply display downward bending branches, giving them an umbrella-like form. But the weeping beech does more than droop; the branches are so twisted that they look like they touched a live electrical socket. Beautiful in spring and summer with lustrous dark green leaves that turn copper in autumn, this tree takes on a new guise in winter when its foliage disappears and its unusual contorted shape casts eerie shadows on the snow. It eventually reaches 50 feet tall with a 40-foot spread. Winter is generally a good time to prune trees, but not so for the beech: In winter and also in spring, it bleeds.

Harry Lauder's walking stick (*Corylus avellana contorta*) is another contorted tree,

OPPOSITE: Anne Busquet's allée of linden trees is limbed up along the driveway, creating a cathedral ceiling and a beautiful entrance to her country house.

even more macabre than the weeping beech. A filbert (or hazelnut) tree, it is mesmerizing for its tangle of corkscrew branches, each one squiggling and twisting like a madcap doodle. I remember being entranced by one many years ago at the entrance to Wave Hill Botanic Garden in the Bronx. When it outgrew its place and was removed, I mourned. My own 12-year-old specimen is still small, but its peculiar-shaped branches are nevertheless intriguing. As for Harry Lauder, he was a Scottish music hall entertainer during the early 1900s. A funny old guy who made the ballad "Roamin' in the Gloamin" famous, he often sang and danced with a twisted walking stick made from the tree.

Yet another twister of a tree, **curly willow (*Salix matsudana*)** has wavy branches and curly twigs that are ideal for cutting and using in arrangements (see page 147). I cut it back to the ground each spring and use the branches, once they have dried out and won't root, to stake other plants in the garden and for flower arrangements. The brightly colored varieties make more of an impact. 'Scarlet Curls' has bright cheery red stems while 'Golden Curls' has orangey branches.

Weeping European birch (*Betula pendula* 'Youngii'), like most white birches, can be recognized by its bark. But unlike its siblings, this smallish variety (about 12 feet tall at maturity) has slender, pendulous branches that curve down to the ground like a floppy mop. It's outstanding with or without its leaves and is a striking specimen in any yard.

Most everybody is familiar with **weeping cherries.** *Prunus yedoensis* 'Shidare Yoshino', the weeper that grows along the banks of the Potomac River in Washington, DC, beckons visitors with clouds of white blossoms in early spring. But long after its flowers have drifted away, the tree's graceful shape commands attention. About 25 feet tall at maturity, its cascading branches billow out another 10 feet or so, to create an umbrella anyone would want to stand under. Other weeping cherries are also prize picks for winter. The one on my front lawn has been turned into a secret clubhouse for visiting kids to play in.

TREES WITH SCULPTURAL SHAPES

Japanese maple (*Acer palmatum*)

Horse chestnut (*Aesculus hyspocostanum*)

Weeping European birch (*Betula pendula* 'Youngii')

American fringe tree (*Chionanthus virginicus*)

Harry Lauder's walking stick (*Corylus avellana contorta*)

European weeping beech (*Fagus sylvatica* 'Pendula')

Carolina silverbell (*Halesia carolina*)

Crape myrtle (*Lagerstroemia indica*)

Tulip tree (*Liriodendron tulipifera*)

Magnolias (*Magnolia* spp.)

Amur cork tree (*Phellodendron amurense*)

London plane tree (*Platanus* × *acerifolia*)

Sargent cherry and weeping cherry (*Prunus sargentii* and *P. yedoensis*)

Willows (*Salix* spp.)

Big leaf linden (*Tilia americana lamur innaeus*)

Weeping, spreading, conical, pyramidal, round,

One of the best trees for year-round beauty is the **Japanese maple (*Acer palmatum*)**. If size is a problem, consider a Japanese maple. They are available as slow-growing petite cultivars, more in keeping with shrubs than trees, and are perfect as a specimen on the front lawn as well as a small shade tree. This extremely popular tree is usually purchased for its finely cut drooping leaves that come in a gamut of shades from deep burgundy to chartreuse. But minus its foliage, it is just as superb, with a distinctive rounded, yet spreading, shape.

Magnolias have beautiful "bones," especially the structure of the **star magnolia (*Magnolia stellata*)**. Of compact stature (only 15 to 20 feet tall and fairly dense), its multistemmed twiggy frame makes a very pretty picture. I planted one in front of my house that I can see and enjoy through my kitchen window while I'm washing dishes. The furry gray flower buds appear during the winter months and open into fragrant, snowy white, star-shaped flowers in early spring. The flowers rarely linger; they are either nipped by frost or wilted by unseasonably warm air. Foliage quickly follows the flowers.

The **Southern magnolia (*M. grandiflora*)** is an evergreen giant. Each leaf is 8 to 10 inches across, glossy green on top and brown suede underneath. When I use them in Christmas decorations, I make sure I tuck in a bunch with some showing the green shiny side and some showing the tan suede side.

The seedpods stand straight up on the branches and are ornamental in late fall when the seeds are bright red. Throughout winter, the brown pods hang on. My magnolia grew from a sapling I brought home in the backseat of my car to a tree 10 feet high and 6 feet wide in less than 10 years. It will mature to about 26 feet high and 13 feet wide.

A Japanese maple is Mother Nature's sculpture. Its curved trunk and weeping branches grab attention wherever it grows. The contrast between its crouching figure and the straight trunks behind it is a lasting winter composition.

or vaselike, there is a shape for every site.

BARKING UP THE RIGHT TREE

Even though I constantly walk around my garden, it wasn't until a dozen years ago that I really began studying the different types of bark. Some looked so smooth that they seemed to have been polished, others were delightfully shaggy, and a few, like my coral bark maples, glowed with a radiance that could be spotted from quite a distance. I began to more closely examine the trees' exposed trunks and branches and now I'm hooked on the intricacies of bark. While I can't identify every tree by its bark (some can), it is easy to recognize the more obvious ones. Recognizing a tree by its bark makes my relationship with nature a little closer. A tree that was only an acquaintance becomes an old friend that I look for whenever I go out.

Bark patterns range from deep vertical fissures to geometric blocks; colors can be gray, brown, yellow, red, or even black. No two barks are identical; indeed, bark is as personal as a fingerprint. But, more to the point, here are some of my favorites trees for using bark to add excitement to your winter garden.

A Tree of a Different Color

Most of us think of bark as brown or gray and rather nondescript, but several trees, such the **red- and yellow-twig dogwoods (*Cornus alba*),** have something way more colorful to offer. In a departure from the familiar flowering dogwood varieties of *Cornus alba*, the red- and yellow-twig dogwoods are more shrublike with lots of branching stems that top out at 4 to 8 feet. In winter, the bark turns a vivid blood red color. *C. alba* 'Siberica' displays stems with a more coral tint that glow like a sunset across a snowy lawn. *C. alba* 'Bud's Yellow' is a different shrub entirely with its bright yellow stems. Since new growth displays better color, both should be pruned yearly.

Among willow species, there are a few excellent options, one of my favorites being ***Salix alba* ssp. *vitellina* 'Britzensis',** sometimes called the **coral embers willow.** It has fiery red stems that are stunning in front of a snowy bank or a row of evergreens. 'Hutchinson's Yellow' has golden yellow branches. Another stunner is *S. myrsinifolia* 'Nigricans', a knockout with shining ebony stems. All three of these should be cut back hard in spring to encourage colorful new growth.

My neighbor's large pollarded yellow-stemmed weeping willow stands near our fence. Pollarding (cutting back branches at the same place each spring) causes large bumpy knots, like knuckles, to form at the top of the tree. It is a tree I "borrow" in

Recognizing a tree by its bark makes my

winter, as it appears to move into our yard as our deciduous trees lose their leaves. Those yellow stems against a gray sky are much appreciated. And the bumpy knobs are so fascinating, they cause me to stare. Although I do wonder: Is pollarding a form of torture for trees?

A real stunner is the **coral-bark maple (*Acer palmatum* 'Sango-Kaku')**. I can't enthuse enough about it. My friend Conni Cross, a talented garden designer, grouped three in front of a holly hedge with hosta at their feet. In winter, the coral branches are brilliant against the deep green of the holly leaves, and the holly berries provide a backdrop of shiny polka dots that dramatize the color even further.

Nature's Abstract Art

Mother Nature, the first proponent of abstract art, has been practicing her craft designing tree trunks. She showcases her subtle but truly fascinating works of art in the textures and patterns of different barks, especially in winter once leaves have dropped.

The shaggy, cinnamon-colored bark on the **paperbark maple (*Acer griseum*)** is a study in abstract expressionism. Some sections are smooth and finely polished, others peel off in thin sheets, and overall it has a mottled appearance that's very intriguing.

The peeling bark of a river birch is best enjoyed up close and personal.

A discourse on bark wouldn't be worth anything without mentioning the glistening trunks of birches, always attention grabbers, and specifically **white birches (*Betula* spp.), river birch (*Betula nigra*), and yellow birch (*Betula lutea*)**. But river birch and yellow birch deliver something extra. River birch has an astonishing bark that peels off the trunk like curled sheets of paper. The color varies from sienna to tan to a creamy orange. A clump positioned where the low winter sun can reflect off its exfoliating bark is a provocative sight.

The yellow or golden birch is an American native that roams the woods in the Adirondacks where our family takes our winter holiday. The tree trunks glow as sunlight streams through the forest. It is a favorite tree for craftsmen who design furniture that showcases its bark.

With its low-lying branches and multiple trunks, **Persian ironwood (*Parrotia persica*)** (about 30 feet tall by 30 feet wide) has a most interesting shape. But if that wasn't enough, its showy bark reveals gray, white, brown, and green shades all at the same time.

relationship with nature a little closer.

DETAILS THAT COUNT

The chilly hand of winter can be cruel: It exposes the skeleton of a garden and even if that skeleton is good, most of us want a little accent or two (or three) to capture our interest. Berries help immensely, but trees can share other gifts such as winged seeds, pods, and other fruits as well. These are the jewels of the winter garden, cherished for their winter stay. The following are some of my favorites.

If you want to know how fast a year goes by, watch a **willow (*Salix*)** grow from a scrawny twig to a fat bush and into a tree. One spring I received a bundle of willow twigs from Wayne Winterrowd, a renowned garden writer and my friend, in Vermont. He wrote, "Willows are such an interesting subject. I don't know why they have so much appeal, but they do. We are now establishing 'willow plantations'—rows of them in out-of-the-way places—on all the country properties we manage, both for their brightly colored twigs in winter and also to provide that elusive "twiggy brush" that is so badly needed for staking some perennials."

I duly planted each as I was told—"Just stick it in the ground, and presto! You have a plant." It couldn't have been simpler. Each twig rooted and sprouted in no time. I enjoyed their pussy willows and brightly colored stems in vases the following winter, but neglected to prune the plants completely back to the ground in spring. Instead of staying as shrubs, they quickly grew into trees and the pussy willows were so far above me I couldn't cut them. The other problem with their rapid growth and their ultimate size is that gardeners often underestimate the space they need.

Not only do willows provide sculptural excitement and color jolts—certain varieties display interesting catkins, too. *Salix hookeriana* produces lovely silvery white pussy willows in mid- to late winter while its sibling, *S. gracilistyla* 'Melanostachys' bears elegant deep purple-black ones with anthers of reddish yellow. A rarer form, *S. × chaenomeloides*,

Lagerstroemia 'Natchez', a hybrid crape myrtle with showy exfoliating cinnamon and red bark, is a sight on a winter day, almost as beautiful as when it's flowering in summer.

The Basics on Bark

To facilitate the recognition of tree species, botanists have classified bark into 18 types. However, a tree may fall into more than one classification as well as move from one to another as it ages. In the first nine classes below, the bark is securely attached to the tree's trunk, while in the subsequent five classes (10 through 14), the bark is peeling. Classes 15 and 16 have warts, technically called *lenticels*, and the last two, Classes 17 and 18, have thorns or spines. Take a purposeful walk through a nearby nursery using the classifications below to help you distinguish differences.

1. Thin, smooth, or bumpy, or occasionally wrinkled
2. Shallow vertical fissures
3. Deep vertical fissures
4. Interlacing ridges
5. Square or rectangular blocks
6. Corky with raised outer bark
7. Cracked with irregular scales
8. Cracked with small to medium scales
9. Scaly with large elongated plates
10. Peeling in thin layers
11. Flaking in asymmetrical patches
12. Peeling in flexible narrow strips
13. Elongated strips
14. Longitudinal ridges
15. Scattered small lenticels or bumps
16. Thin raised horizontal lines
17. Conical spines
18. Needlelike spines

TREES WITH INTERESTING BARK

Thorny bark: Castor, hawthorn, osage orange

Furrowed bark: Amur cork, black walnut, mulberry, sassafrass, sweet gum, tulip tree

Flaking or peeling bark: Chinese elm, paperbark maple, Persian ironwood, London plane tree, river birch, Russian olive

Smooth bark: Beech, Korean mountain ash, saucer magnolia, serviceberry, yellowwood

Colored bark: Beech (gray), canoe birch (white), coral-bark maple (coral), crape myrtle 'Natchez' (cinnamon), cucumber tree (gray), European white birch (white), gray birch (white), Japanese stewartia (tan to gray camouflage pattern), Kentucky coffee tree (black), paperbark cherry (red), Sargent cherry (red to brown), saucer magnolia (grey), tartarian dogwood (yellow, coral, red), white alder (white to brown), white poplar (greenish white), willow (red, yellow) the white pussy willow, is a favorite of Wayne, my Vermont friend; he named his culti-var 'White Kittens'. I'll have to see if I can snip a twig next time I visit him. All can be forced for splendid indoor bouquets.

Catalpa (*Catalpa speciosa*), a fairly large spreading tree, shows off clusters of white bell-shaped flowers with purple streaks in spring, followed by 8- to 14-inch-long capsules filled with winged seeds. The capsules frequently hold on through the winter months, hanging down through the branches like bunches of skinny brown beans.

Even though the **golden rain tree (*Koelreuteria paniculata*)** offers up cheerful yellow flowers in later summer and fall, it's best known for its bundles of 2-inch pinkish brown seedpods suspended from the end of its branches. The papery pods resemble tiny balloons that start out green, blush pink, then dry to a warm brown. They hang decoratively all through the winter months. The tree ultimately reaches 20 to 30 feet tall with a spread of 10 to 20 feet.

The large hardwood **sweet gum (*Liquidambar styraciflua*)** is noted for its rapid growth up to 60 or 70 feet, lovely autumn color, and prickly brown fruits. These hard, spiny spheres, about the size of golf balls, dangle from the trees after the leaves have fallen. I know gardeners who consider the balls messy when they drop to the ground and hate raking them up—but not I! I collect them to display in a bowl mixed with pinecones for the holidays and wire some into wreaths.

The **gray alder (*Alnus incana*)**, a small, frost-resistant tree, is unique in that it bears both male and female catkins on the same tree. Both types of catkins dangle in clusters long after the tree's leaves have disappeared; the male ones are long and reddish brown, while the females resemble small pine cones.

I value **flowering crab apples (*Malus* spp.)** as much for their colorful fruits as their spring flowers. Beginning in September the fruits appear and continue to ripen through November. Many crab apples hold onto their fruit through most of winter. Freezing even enhances the color of some berries. Although red and orange are commonly grown, the fruit of other varieties comes in a wondrous array from pale lime to bright yellow and gold through shades of burgundy and purple.

M. 'Donald Wyman' and *M. sargentii* have lived for

TREES WITH DECORATIVE WINTER FRUITS

Berries: Crab apple (red, yellow, green), hawthorn (red), mountain ash (yellow, orange, red), mulberry (pink, red, purple), serviceberry (red, purple)

Pods: Catalpa (brown), golden rain tree (pink, orange), redbud (pinkish brown), silk tree (gray-brown)

Nuts or ball-like fruit: Horse chestnut or buckeye (brown), oak (brown), osage orange (yellowish green), pecan (brown), plane tree (brown), sweet gum (green turning brown), walnut (brown)

Catkins: Gray alder (reddish brown and brown), willow (silver, dark purple)

Mother Nature showcases her subtle works of

20 years on my front lawn and both matured into small trees with graceful umbrella shapes and abundant flowers and red fruit. The red fruit of 'Sugartyme' persists all winter, too, but I admit I planted it for its fragrant white spring blooms. 'Red Jade' is an excellent weeping cultivar, and 'Christmas Holly' is a small rounded tree with so much fruit in December that it resembles a holly. 'Winter Gold' is one of the best for bright yellow fruits.

So keep these suggestions in mind the next time you're in the market for a new tree or two. And remember to consider rate of growth and eventual size. London plane trees, for example, soar up rather quickly; an 8- or 10-footer may reach 35 feet after 10 years. (Our plane tree is my children's favorite, as they've spent many a happy time climbing up into it. We've used it often as a backdrop for family portraits, with some kids in its branches.) A ginkgo of roughly the same size planted at the same time will only hit 20 feet. But these tough trees can withstand the abuse of New York City sidewalks, drought, and heat.

The red fruit of crab apple trees adds color to the winter landscape. 'Sugartyme', pictured above, has fragrant flowers in spring that cling all winter.

THE LAST LAUGH

Elvin McDonald, a friend who lives in Iowa, summed up my garden's progress when he remarked, "Haven't gardeners always started with annuals and ended up planting trees?" His maternal grandfather planted an orchard when he was in his seventies, and the townsfolk made fun of him. But Elvin's grandfather had the last laugh, dying at age 96 after the orchard itself had gone into decline. Furnishing the garden with trees is a great investment. They never need slipcovers and only get better with age.

art in the textures and patterns of different barks.

Colorful Conifers and Broadleaf Evergreens

When we bought our house 30 years ago, there were no foundation plantings. Honeysuckle and English ivy covered the house, roof, and even the windows. It was known as the spook house—no one could see in or out. After cutting

OPPOSITE: The rock alpine garden at the Denver Botanic Garden has a mixture of conifers and deciduous trees that makes a pleasing background composition in any season of the year.

back the ivy and honeysuckle, we added foundation plantings. After all, it's the American way. Foundations, I thought, like underwear, were not meant to be seen. I now know better.

Not knowing I had other choices, I added clumps of rhododendron, pieris, and azalea and wove them together with pachysandra. My husband planted a variegated euonymus hedge under the windows. Over the years I added flowers—roses that climb up and bloom over the ivy in summer, an osmanthus that perfumes the front walk in fall, a star magnolia and a dogwood that add spring bloom. Tree peonies and deciduous peonies alleviate the rectangular, austerely pruned hedge. A decade passed before I planted specifically for winter, adding bulbs galore in the lawn and the pachysandra.

But I hadn't noticed conifers were missing until the next decade, when I wanted an assortment of gold and blue conifer cuttings to embellish my Christmas decorations. They were hard to find in the flower market, so I planted a few of my own.

As deciduous plants nap, conifers move to the forefront, flaunting myriad shades of green, as well as silver, gold, and blue. Their colorful tapestry warms a winter garden.

About the same time, my friend Conni Cross, a nursery owner, bluntly told me to connect the dots—those specimen trees and shrubs I'd surrounded with circles of groundcover on my front lawn. One or two specimens were fine, but over the years I'd added close to a dozen. Once she said it, I knew it was true.

So I began connecting the trees. A *Franklinia*, an ornamental cherry, and a dove tree (*Davidia*) that once stood alone are now included within my new winter bed. It is an island planting with specimen conifers such as *Picea orientalis* 'Skyland' and *Chamaecyparis nootkatensis* 'Pendula' as focal points and masses of mounding evergreen groundcovers including *Nandina* 'Woods' Dwarf', *Osmanthus* 'Goshiki', *Chamaecyparis* 'Gold Mop', and *Leucothoe* 'Scarletta' and 'Rainbow' holding it all together. The placement is perfect, along the driveway across from the front door where I can enjoy the rich tapestry of color on a daily basis year-round.

OPPOSITE: The collection of conifers in Conni Cross's garden adds color to every season. The blue spruce and green juniper rugs are set off by the glow of golden chamaecyparis.

THE CULT OF THE CONIFER

Most of us are familiar with conifers—after all, this category includes Christmas trees—but may not realize the name means *cone bearer*, whether they are common pinecones or the berrylike fruits of juniper. Typically conifers are evergreen with foliage that is needlelike as in pines, flat and linear as in yews, or small and scalelike as in arborvitae. Foliage can be prickly or soft to the touch. Conifers may grow upright as trees, broad and rounded as shrubs, or prostrate as groundcovers.

Besides lending texture and substance to the winter garden, conifers deliver a dash of color. As deciduous plants nap, conifers move to the forefront, flaunting myriad shades of green, as well as silver, gold, and blue. Golden arborvitae, for instance, can't be beat for giving definition to winter's pared-down palette. And where would we be without blue spruce?

The plants I list in this chapter are only a sampling of the many cultivars available for home gardens. Once you know the look you want—a small golden conifer, a furry blue rug, a pencil thin green exclamation mark—check your local nursery and if need be substitute a readily available cultivar that fills the bill. This list is to jump-start your creative juices and help unleash your imagination.

THE SCENT OF CHRISTMAS

In our camp in the Adirondacks, we have several small pillows stuffed with dried balsam that I tuck behind the larger pillows on the sofa. Unknowingly, guests sit down and lean back against the pillows, releasing the wonderful, fresh woodsy scent. Their reaction is always the same. They comment on the wonderful smell of the woods and how marvelous it is that they can even pick up the aroma sitting inside. They haven't a clue about the perfumed pillows and assume the balsam scent is seeping in under the doors and around the window frames.

Variety: The Spice of Life

Just as a good hostess knows that the key to a great party is an interesting mix of guests, a gardener knows that a great garden also relies on variety. Happily, conifers come in all shapes, sizes, and personalities. Some such as the **Oriental spruce 'Skyland' (*Picea orientalis* 'Skyland')** and the **golden Atlas cedar (*Cedrus atlantica* 'Aurea')** are like elegant guests arriving for a black-tie party in fur coats and golden ball gowns. There is no getting around how they dress up a garden, adding a more formal and polished appearance. Then there are the show-offs, a bit overdressed and full of themselves. But every garden, like every party, needs this kind of personality. **'Ellwoodii' Lawson false cypress (*Chamaecyparis lawsoniana* 'Ellwoodii')** is tall, thin, and wonderfully elegant but slightly over done. A classic beauty, **false cypress (*C. obtusa* 'Crippsii')** has brilliant yellow sprays artfully arranged in layers like Cinderella's ball gown. The **blue spruce** is the dowager Queen Mother, full figured and richly draped in wavy fir.

Some are short and squat. Dusted with snow and swaying with the wind, a **dwarf**

OPPOSITE: *Chamaecyparis nootkatensis* 'Pendula' is so furry that it reminds me of the Cookie Monster standing at attention in the garden.

Hinoki cypress 'Nana Gracilis' waddles like a toddler in a snowsuit.

And we mustn't forget the eccentrics, such as ***Chamaecyparis nootkatensis*** that looks like it's waving its arms and wearing a witch's hat or *C.* 'Pendula', a weeper that reminds me of Cookie Monster, or ***Abies alba* 'Green Spiral',** a tall skinny morose fir with droopy branches. Squint at conifers in the garden on a foggy winter day and you'll get the picture. Let your imagination go and the figures might dance. Good gardeners are skilled at seeing what could be rather than what is.

The Midas Touch

Gold in any form is eye-catching. Your eye sees yellow before any other color. It attracts and dominates. Think of how a spotlight lights a stage or how intense sunlight dazzles and you'll get the point.

Golden foliage warms up the garden, especially

Golden foliage warms up the garden, especially on cold, dark days. It lets the sunshine in. Whenever I see the glow from the **Oriental spruce 'Skyland' (*Picea orientalis* 'Skyland')** in my island planting, it is as if the sun unexpectedly peeked out from behind dark clouds. Consequently, gold needs to be used with restraint. It can be gaudy if too many golden plants are strewn about. Your eye struggles to connect the dots without enjoying the view. I use gold as a deliberate focal point to emphasize a garden feature or to lighten a dark area, like sparks to light up its neighbors.

Gardener's gold may be chartreuse, sulfur, citron, lemon, shiny, or matte. And consider this: The saturation of the color often depends on the amount of direct sun the plant receives. The gleam may dim if planted in dense shade; on the other hand, some golden foliage may scorch in full sun. Check descriptions carefully for cultivars that are prone to scorching.

My selects for gilding the garden include a few false cypress such as the classic

Gold conifers come in many shapes and sizes. All of them bring a little sunshine to earth on a gray day.
ABOVE, LEFT TO RIGHT: *Chamaecyparis obtusa* 'Crippsii' surrounded by forget-me-nots; *Chamaecyparis pisifera* 'Compacta Variegata'.
OPPOSITE, LEFT TO RIGHT: A golden form of *Juniperus chinensis*; Oriental spruce 'Skyland'.

on cold, dark days. It lets the sunshine in.

golden beauty *Chamaecyparis obtusa* 'Crippsii', with its long needles held in large frond-like, feathery branches, ruffled in horizontal layers. *C. obtusa* 'Nana Aurea' is a dwarf slow-grower with bright gold new foliage that contrasts with its mature greenish yellow, ruffled foliage. It slips easily into a small space. *C. pisifera* 'Filifera Aurea' impresses with its intensity. The threadlike drooping foliage reminds me of golden yarns unraveling from a shawl. **Cedrus libani 'Aurea'**, the yellow-needled atlas cedar, brightens winter. Cedars, firs, and arborvitae also offer golden gems for the garden.

If you are wary of overgilding, there are conifers that change to yellow only in December. **Pinus sylvestris 'Gold Coin', 'Gold Metal', and 'Aurea'** are three bushy pine wonders that brighten as the season darkens. For dwarf varieties, **P. mugo 'Winter Gold' and 'Ophir'** are good choices. **Abies nordmanniana 'Golden Spreader'** is a fir ground-hugger. Since these conifers are such chameleons, you aren't stuck with the gold scheme year-round.

Polishing the Silver

I never knew Ellen Willmott and yet her ghost haunts us all. As the story goes, she was a legendary gardener and an eccentric lady—beautiful in her youth, too rich for her own good, and not one to trouble herself about what other people thought. In the early 1900s, when she thought no one was looking, Miss Willmott scattered the seeds of **sea holly (*Eryngium giganteum*)** in gardens of friends and neighbors. Many scratched their heads after her visits, wondering how the thistly silver-blue rosettes popped up in their beds and borders, but no one complained and the plants thrived beautifully. Soon the ethereal plants became known as Miss Willmott's ghost, and they're still referred to this way today.

> ## SINGING THE BLUES
> Blue conifers have a waxy coating on their needles that protects them from air pollution. So if you garden in a polluted area, choose a blue cultivar of fir, cedar, cypress, juniper, spruce, or pine.

Miss Willmott's mission, as she saw it, was to rectify the lack of silver thistles in the garden. In truth, she had the right idea—many a garden needs polishing. (The most popular perennials that can be counted on to provide a silver accent are lavender and lamb's ear. They can even be picked in the snow and mixed with other greens for an indoor arrangement.) Thankfully, there are many conifers that provide a glittery sheen.

Frasier fir (*Abies fraseri*) is a tall American native from the Allegheny Mountains. Their needles are soft, shiny, and dark green on top with a silver sheen on the underside. Nurserymen designated it the "Cadillac of Christmas Trees," but its appeal, like the Cadillac, is being challenged by other firs that hold onto their needles for a longer time. Still, it's Frasier fir tips that are most used in Christmas wreaths.

Cedrus deodara 'Silver Mist' is a cedar that justifies its name with long, silvery new growth as soft as a well-loved blanket. Since the mature foliage is a gray green, the overall effect is of burnished pewter. The **false cypress 'Snowflake'** (*Chamaecyparis obtusa* **'Snowflake'**) is also well-labeled. The grayish foliage of this dwarf cypress is speckled with cream, as if a light snowfall had dusted it gently. Bolder and much more silvery in tone is *Juniperus conferta* **'Silver Mist'**. This dwarf juniper, only 12 inches high, is splendid as a groundcover. The slate foliage, flushed with white, mimics a mound of molten silver.

But my favorite gleamer is the **Silver Curls Korean fir** (*Abies koreana* **'Silberlocke'**). This upright conical tree is a slow grower, but it can reach 25 feet. It has slightly curled fluorescent blue needles lit up by silvery linings. I planted a trio along the driveway, and they look sensational holding up clusters of purple cones in early winter. By late January the cones have dried to tan, and by February they have broken apart and fallen off. ('Aurea', a newer gold-needled introduction, was worth waiting for. It is available in specialty catalogs in a small size.)

Rhapsody in Blue

Blue is America's top color for decorating and its popularity extends to the garden. Blue flowers are always bestsellers, and foliage tinged with the hue can tranquilize the most chaotic border. Perhaps because our eyes can distinguish many different shades of blue, the color works especially well in a bleak winter scenario. Nuances in shading take on more intensity; the blue seems bluer against the snow and shows up splendidly against dark evergreens.

Juniperus squamata **'Blue Star'** is a compact juniper with foliage so intensely blue it can appear turquoise when the sun's rays light it up. Since it grows into tight, tufted mounds, I like to see it en masse as a groundcover. Not quite as brazen, but still bewitching, is the fine-textured blue foliage of the **false cypress 'Bluefeathers'** (*Chamaecyparis obtusa* **'Bluefeathers'**) and the soft, gray blue needles of the **dwarf white pine 'Blue Mist'** (*Pinus strobus* **'Blue Mist'**).

Of course, the bluest of the blues occurs in **Colorado blue spruce**. *Picea pungens* 'Koster' is a classic upright conical tree with silver blue needles, but newer cultivars are even more azure. 'Hoopsi' bears long, thick needles in vivid cerulean; 'Moerheim' is a splendid powdery blue.

A close-up of Silver Curls Korean fir shows the blue needles curled along the stem revealing their silver linings.

Abies koreana 'Starker's Dwarf' hugs the ground when it is young. As it ages, it becomes conical. It produces cones at an early age.

Good Things Come in Small Packages

Thanks to my garden designer friend Conni, I've been introduced to a slew of petite, even tiny, conifers. Some are dwarf versions of their taller siblings; others are species in and of themselves. These little guys, ranging from a wee 12 inches to a more substantial 6 feet, have personalities much, much bigger than their size.

Indeed, for personality plus, you can't beat the **Hinoki false cypress (*Chamaecyparis obtusa*)**. It has so many cultivars that it's hard to believe they belong to the same species. 'Nana', a miniature flat-topped dome, consists of fans of dark green foliage arranged in tiers. 'Gold Drop', with flattened coppery green needles, begins as a pudgy toddler then slims down as it reaches its teens. 'Spiralis' lives up to its name with twisted foliage on a small, conical form. None of these top out at more than 3 feet.

While most firs (*Abies* spp.) grow into stately trees, their smaller cousins also pack a wallop. ***A. balsamea* 'Nana'** doesn't reach more than 2 feet high, but it holds the scent of Christmas in its needles. ***A. concolor* 'Compacta'** is a dwarf white fir with lovely grayish blue needles on a 4- to 6-foot form. It makes a great solo specimen. *A. koreana* 'Starker's Dwarf' has dark glossy green foliage and grows densely, hugging the ground and becoming conical with age.

Although the tall, stately varieties of **arborvitae (*Thuja* spp.)** are extremely popular here in the Northeast, I'm very fond of some of the shorter ones. *T. occidentalis* 'Teddy' reminds me of my Westie, also named Teddy. It's a dense little ball of grayish green that's so soft you want to pet it. The egg-shaped *T. orientalis* 'Rosedalis' is a real changeling: yellow in spring, sea green in summer, and plum in winter. Even at age 15, it won't be more than 3 feet tall.

DWARFS MASQUERADING AS GIANTS

Be forewarned that a dwarf conifer can be misleading. If you plant a dwarf conifer near your house expecting it to stay small, you could be dearly mistaken. Dwarf only means that the cultivar does not reach the size of its parent. If the parent is 80 feet tall, a dwarf cultivar might reach 40 feet, which could be way too big for the spot you chose.

Big Can Be Better

As adorable as the mini conifers may be, there's no dismissing the fact that sometimes you need a strong presence. Large trees, either tall and skinny or huge and spreading, can create a privacy screen, hide a bad view, or create a needed focal point. I don't know what I'd do without the three big cedars, **Cedrus atlantica 'Glauca',** that stand guard at the back of my rose garden. Their main duty is to look great while blocking out the neighbors' house. They give new definition to the word "grandeur." With massive trunks and horizontal branches, they're excellent specimen plantings.

When young, *C. atlantica* 'Glauca' is as lean as a model, but it ages into a grand dame with a girth that casts dense shade. At 60 feet tall with a 40-foot spread, this diva has the extra plus of shimmering, narrow blue needles. The cedars of Lebanon are similar but slower growing.

Why the genus *Chamaecyparis* is called false cypress rather than having its own name seems strange to me, but botanists can be a strange group. These conifers are distinguished from true cypress (*Cupressus*) by their flattened, frondlike sprays of foliage and greater hardiness. They are easily identified by a nodding leader. Every other year they shed their inner needles. The species *C. lawsoniana* offers many distinguished choices. *The Manual of Cultivated Conifers* lists 238 lawsoniana cultivars. 'Columnaris' has a small narrow shape with densely packed flat, blue gray branches. At 15 to 20 feet high, it works well as a hedge. 'Ellwoodii' is equally svelte, but taller and decidedly formal. Petite plants in 4-inch pots are offered in December at many nurseries for both indoor settings and outdoor window boxes. 'Intertexta' has a different shape entirely—wider, more open, with drooping branches and large fans of dark green foliage.

Of course, if I'm talking big, I need to talk about **spruces (Picea spp.).** In addition to the splendid Colorado blues that I mentioned before, **P. pungens 'Iseli Fastigiate'** is a top-notch choice if space is tight and a vertical is needed. It makes a nice narrow column that grows up instead of out. The steel blue color has a cool industrial look. **P. orientalis,** the Oriental spruce, is also worth looking into. This statuesque beauty has dense branches all the way down to the ground.

Cedrus atlantica 'Glauca' is a majestic conifer. It is skinny when young and bulks up as it ages.

Weepers and Spreaders

I can't remember the first weeping conifer that caught my attention, but I do recall being fascinated by *Picea abies* **'Pendula'**, a dwarf weeping spruce. Creeping this way and that over the soil, it looks a bit like an octopus—but with many more arms. I later saw it staked to grow upright to about 5 feet with its branches tumbling down over an arbor; that's the way I like it best. What an intriguing plant!

Hemlocks (*Tsuga* spp.) are a common sight in my northeastern part of the United States. 'Bennet' is a miniature with lime green needles and arching branches that lie in symmetrical layers. 'Jeddolah' looks like a giant bird's nest (2 feet by 3 feet), right down to a depression in the center.

The ***Chamaecyparis obtusa*** species includes a few spreaders, but 'Pygmaea Aurescens' might be the most striking. This broad bush, about $1\frac{1}{2}$ feet by 3 feet, has loose sprays of olive foliage that turn a rich copper color in winter. A cousin, *C. pisifera* 'Gold Mop', also known as 'Mops' and 'Golden Mops', is a floppy fellow,

One of my garden's miracles is that bulbs planted under the prickly needles of these junipers bloom without a scratch.

dressed in chartreuse threadlike fir. A fast grower, it only reaches 5 feet with a wider spread that does mimic a very large mop.

For fabulous low-maintenance groundcovers, I depend on the **rug junipers (*Juniperus horizontalis*)**. An assortment of different hues can be woven together for a tantalizing tapestry. 'Bar Harbor', 'Blue Chip', and 'Wiltonii' are bluish; 'Emerald Spreader' and 'Heidi' show shades of gray green; 'Lime Glow' and 'Mother Lode' gleam with gold. If all these provide too much color, green shades are also available. 'Prince of Wales' is a stunner that takes on a sophisticated plum cast in winter. The **shore junipers (*J. conferta*)** also scamper along the ground in a gamut of tones from the bright

OPPOSITE: A blue rug juniper colorfully carpets the ground and requires little if any maintenance.

blue of 'Blue Lagoon' to the sunny yellow of 'Sunsplash', with the pewter tone of 'Silver Mist' in between. Lucky for me, one of my garden's miracles is that bulbs planted under the prickly needles of these junipers come through and bloom without a scratch. They are in a league of their own.

Out-of-the-Ordinary Conifers

Maybe I'm a pushover for the unusual, but there are some conifers that are worth planting just because they're so different. Sometimes it's their bark that sets them apart, other times it's their needles or their shape, but they add an element of whimsy or strangeness that gives a garden another layer of richness.

Rather surprisingly, it's the oh-so-familiar pine that offers some of the oddest selections. **Lacebark pine (*Pinus bungeana*)** is better known for its colorful peeling bark than its olive green needles. The bark flakes at random, creating a crazy quilt of white, yellow, purple, brown, and green. Since the branches start near the base, it's a good idea to remove the lower ones to enjoy the beauty of the trunk.

I'm also fascinated by **Japanese black pine (*Pinus thunbergii*)**. Its slightly twisted branches reach out horizontally to form irregular shapes and in winter the dark green needles are crowned by large silver "candles"—new upright shoots—that are as fetching as flowers.

For something decidedly weird, look no further than the **dragon's eye pine (*P. densiflora* 'Oculus-draconis')**. Its name sounds like one from *Harry Potter* and its curious form displays pairs of wide yellow bands on its 5-inch green needles. Another family member, *P. wallichiana* 'Umbraculifera', a small dome-shaped bush, has kinked needles and banana-shaped cones. Talk about strange relatives!

Not related to the pines but sharing a name, **Japanese umbrella pine (*Sciadopitys verticillata*)** is too often overlooked. A dense conical tree when young, it grows looser and broader as it matures and can end up 25 to 40 feet tall and half as wide. The needles are long, glossy, dark green, and surprisingly soft to the touch. Supposedly, the whorls of needles resemble the spokes of an umbrella, but I think that's a stretch. My three 'Wintergreen' grow so perfectly with needles so shiny that they could be mistaken for plastic. 'Anne Hadow' is a prized form, noted for its golden yellow nee-

> ### ALL WRAPPED UP
>
> Some gardeners in northern areas wrap conifers in burlap to keep their branches close to their trunks so they can't be snapped off by the weight of falling snow and ice.
>
> Deedee Wigmore, an expert gardener in the Adirondacks, takes it a step further. After covering her conifers with burlap, she ties them up with red ribbons and lights. She also adds lights to the pergola behind her garden, thus turning a necessity into a gorgeous holiday decoration.

Yews can be seen in public gardens clipped

dles; 'Jim Cross', named after a close friend of mine and one of the best nurserymen who ever lived, retains its columnar shape.

Another distinctive conifer is *Tsuga canadensis* **'Pendula'**, a hemlock that's a notable exception to the usual conical form. In 10 years' time it will grow into a flat-topped dome 3 feet tall and twice as wide with overlapping, drooping branches. The 75-year-old specimens at the New York Botanical Garden look like one-room cottages. After ducking under their branches, you can stand up straight and walk around. Of course, they can be kept tidy for a smaller garden with judicious pruning.

Last, but definitely not least, are the yews, worth mentioning because they can be easily sheared into boxes, balls, and other forms. Yews are also the favorite of topiary artists and can be seen in public gardens clipped into a veritable zoo of comical creatures. Of the seven species, **English yew (*Taxus baccata*)** is the most widely used. 'Davie' is a miniature, a squat rounded form with dark green needles that change to amber bronze in winter. 'Semperaurea', a medium bush with short ascending branches, presents new needles in a mellow yellow that morph into rust as they mature.

The golden Japanese umbrella pine's long shiny needles spiral around the stem so perfectly that they almost look like they are plastic.

into a veritable zoo of comical creatures.

The New York Botanical Garden's Top 10 Conifers

Todd Forest, the associate vice president for Horticulture and Living Collections at the New York Botanical Garden, shares his expertise in the concise tip sheets he writes for garden visitors.

He recommends that conifers be planted in spring or fall in full sun with good garden soil, although he notes that hemlock, plum yew, and yew are very shade tolerant. True cedars, chamaecyparis, arborvitae, and many spruces and firs withstand light shade, but pines, larches, and cypresses grow best in full sun.

A conifer requires a planting hole three times the width of and the same depth as its container or root-ball. The root crown should be set at or slightly above grade level. Before planting, gently remove the conifer from its container and loosen its root-ball. On field-dug specimens, remove the burlap and wire wrapping.

Add compost to the backfill to improve root growth. Use excess backfill to create a low berm around the planting hole to hold water to soak into the root-ball. (For poorly drained sites, choose bald cypress, dawn redwood, or swamp white cedar. Dig a wider than usual hole and plant in a mound 3 to 4 inches above the original grade.)

Upright conifers need staking for a year after planting. All newly planted conifers should receive an inch of water, whether from a hose or Mother Nature, each week.

Todd recommends using miniature and dwarf conifers in rock gardens and for foundation plantings and intermediate and large conifers as specimens and screens. When asked to choose his favorites from the more than 200 different varieties he has grown, he listed the 10 at right.

1. *Abies Koreana* 'Silberlocke' (Silver Curls Korean fir)

2. *Cedrus atlantica* 'Glauca' (weeping blue Atlas cedar)

3. *Chamaecyparis nootkatensis* 'Pendula' (weeping Nootka cypress)

4. *Chamaecyparis obtusa* 'Nana Gracilis' (dwarf Hinoki cypress)

5. *Juniperus horizontalis* 'Lime Glow' (golden spreading juniper)

6. *Picea pungens* 'R. H. Montgomery' (dwarf blue Colorado spruce)

7. *Pinus strobus* 'Sea Urchin' (miniature eastern white pine)

8. *Pinus wallichiana* 'Zebrina' (variegated Himalayan pine)

9. *Sciadopitys verticillata* 'Wintergreen' (Japanese umbrella pine)

10. *Thuja* 'Green Giant' (green giant arborvitae)

OPPOSITE: A mature weeping blue Atlas cedar majestically sits on the lawn and invites visitors to sit under its branches at Planting Fields Arboretum on Long Island.

BROADLEAF EVERGREENS AND GROUNDCOVERS

Hollies, rhododendrons, azaleas, and other broadleaf evergreens are seldom recognized for their astounding feats in the winter garden; ditto for evergreen groundcovers. Instead, we applaud the winter-blooming shrubs, bulbs, and the stately conifers, overlooking the stalwarts that do so much to contribute to a winter landscape's success. These are the bit players that pull the garden together and make the stars shine.

Hail to the Hollies

Come December, boughs of holly are seen in all the best places—wreathing front doors, draping fireplaces, and even gracing dinner tables. And no wonder, with its shiny, porcelain-like leaves and red berries, it brings holiday cheer. Yet, with December's passing, so do all thoughts of holly. I'm all for more hollies in more gardens. Glorious in the fall with white, cream, red, orange, or yellow berries, they are a favorite food of many birds. In winter, holly does double duty, moving indoors for the holidays and, at the same time, brightening the outdoor landscape. Spring is best remembered for holly's fragrant clusters of small white flowers. In summer, hollies win the gardeners' praise and respect with their ability to keep their great looks while withstanding heat and drought.

Here in the Northeast, **American holly (*Ilex opaca*)** flourishes in forests and decorates many suburban yards. What some gardeners don't realize, however, is that hollies can bear cream, black, orange, or yellow fruit as well as the familiar scarlet. Bushes studded with these gleaming gems are an unexpected delight. I particularly like 'Lake City' whose spinach green leaves morph to bronze in winter—stunning against its orange fruit.

For red berries, the list is almost limitless. A smart choice is the 2003 Holly of the Year, 'Satyr Hill'—the berries are nice and fat and lipstick red and last all

A LITTLE HISTORY LESSON

Holly is native to every continent except Antarctica. Its pale hard wood has been dyed black as a substitute for ebony piano keys. It also has a rich and compelling history of use in medicine, science, magic, and superstition. Some of the more interesting lore involves the druids, priests of ancient Britain. They first decorated their dwellings with holly (the thorny plants were believed to repel all evil spirits), then the Christians followed their example.

In Christian legend the berries of holly were stained red from the wounds of Christ. Superstitions later claimed if a holly outside a home was smooth, it was a she-holly and the woman ran the house. If it was prickly, it was a he-holly and the man was in charge. Another superstition held that it was decidedly unlucky to leave holly decorations up after New Year's Day.

One of the many joys of planting a holly is having

winter until the robins appear and feast on them in spring. 'Satyr Hill' grows faster than most hollies and has a compact upright habit, which means it can hold its own solo as a specimen plant or strut its stuff in a hedge or mixed border.

The bright berries of *Ilex opaca* 'Ms. Courtney' feed the birds and brighten the view. Branches are also good for cutting and bringing indoors for holiday decorations.

Hollies are easy to grow, low maintenance, drought-tolerant, and long-lived. Their slow growth, 6 to 12 inches a year, means they only need occasional pruning and won't quickly outgrow their place. The degree of hardiness varies with the specific holly. English hollies need a mild climate (Oregon is perfect), while among the 30 or so species of American hollies, there are choice cultivars for each zone.

Hollies are available in almost any size and shape—spreading, columnar, and vaselike to mention a few—making it easy to fit them into the landscape. As foundation plantings, hollies are compatible with most architectural styles and materials. They are the most beautiful plants for hedges, screens, or barriers, yet are equally at home in tubs on terraces. With today's interest in winter gardens, consider planting a backbone of holly as a stage for the hellebores, primroses, snowdrops, winter aconite, and witch hazels you'd like to showcase.

One of the many joys of planting a holly is having your own supply for indoor arrangements. The English holly, commonly sold for Christmas decorations, is harvested in Oregon up to 5 weeks before it is sold. Although treated with chemicals to retard wilting and leaf drop, it often withers quickly. Unique hollies picked from one's own garden are fresher and available anytime.

your own supply for indoor arrangements.

The Sex Life of a Holly

The deliciously fragrant flowers of holly hold a sweet nectar that keeps the bees happily pollinating. If you wet your finger and draw it across the berry in the flower's center, you too can taste the sweet sap that flavors holly honey.

While I rarely concern myself with the sex life of plants, with holly I must. A female holly tree needs a male nearby to bear fruit. Both flower in spring, the only time they can be easily told apart. Male flowers have pollen, while females have a pistil resembling a small green berry in their center. When the female flowers are pollinated, they develop into the eye-catching berries of fall. An unpollinated female drops her fruit. A male easily produces enough pollen to keep 10 to 20 females in fruit, even if some of them live a quarter of a mile away. So, if there is a male holly nearby, you need not plant one. 'Jersey Prince' is thought to be the best male pollinator for American holly trees, and 'Jim Dandy' is the guy for winterberry shrubs.

Favorites and Not So Familiar Favorites

Rhododendron and azalea are so well-known for their evergreen leaves, I won't dwell on them too much. But I do want to say that I'd like to see the **Yakushima rhododendron (_Rhododendron yakushimanum_)** planted more often. It is a slow-growing dense shrub, ideal for both borders and foundation planting, with long and very narrow oval leaves. The leaves' undersides are covered in a silvery, woolly pubescence that slows evaporation, and maybe because of this they don't seem to suffer the "winter droops" as much as other rhodies do. Their flowers are beautiful, too, rose or red in bud and bleaching to white when they open. 'Mist Maiden' grows faster and larger than the species, reaching 5 feet by 5 feet.

As for **azaleas**, there are enough to satisfy every size and color requirement, and if you do a little homework, you can have cultivars that bloom from early May into July. But since we're concentrating on winter interest, I recommend 'Karen', a violet-flowering variety whose foliage becomes a rich burgundy in fall and stays that way through the colder months. 'Girard Variegated Hot Shot' has white-flecked leaves that take on pink and magenta tints come autumn. As if the fabulous foliage wasn't outstanding enough, the flowers are a blazing crimson that start to sizzle in late May.

Holly comes in many different guises.
OPPOSITE, CLOCKWISE FROM TOP LEFT: _Ilex_ 'Honey Maid', _I. verticillata_ 'Aurantiaca', _I. aquifolium_ 'Alba-marginata', _I. verticillata_ 'Winter Red', _I. aquifolium_ 'Winter Queen', and last but not least, a holly look-alike, _Osmanthus_ 'Goshiki'
BELOW: Yakushima rhododendron

Pieris japonica dangles colorful buds all winter before opening them in late March.
OPPOSITE: Firethorn berries are held along prickly branches making them difficult to cut and bring indoors.

Year-Round Beauty

A winter wonder with all-season appeal is **Pieris japonica,** sometimes referred to as lily-of-the-valley shrub. Come early March, this popular evergreen tantalizes with extravagant dangles (think 6 inches long!) of tiny, urn-shaped blossoms. To me, these tassels resemble Victorian beaded brooches, pinned on each and every branch, so that the shrub is almost covered in jewels. The blooms start to appear during the first thaw, usually late February or early March, and the sight of these lustrous pearls against the glossy green leaves creates a spectacular image. But even in tight bud, they show their color. I frequently clip stems to embellish Christmas wreaths, bouquets, and mantels.

Pieris is usually touted as a great foundation plant—and it is—but a clutch of them grouped together in an island bed can be quite striking. The added attraction is that new foliage that appears in spring is red, bronze, or even pink, and the buds that appear in autumn deliver a red or pink color punch. The most familiar varieties, such as 'White Cascade', boast ivory blossoms, but I like to grow those with pink or rose blooms. Some of my favorites include 'Flamingo' with deep pink flowers and 'Daisen' with red flowers. And I must mention 'Valley Valentine'. This petite beauty, only 4 feet tall, displays dusty red blossoms and is lovely tucked into a border.

A Showgirl

Another popular berried treasure is **pyracantha,** commonly called firethorn. These carefree shrubs, which are blanketed with white blossoms in spring, come into their own in fall and winter with a dazzling display of orangey-red berries. I know some gardeners feel the color is rather garish, but I say go for it. When everything around you is in shades of gray and brown, you need something bold and brash. I've trained a bush to scramble up the front of the house where it looks like a neon sculpture—a little Las Vegas maybe, but lots of fun.

I must admit however that pyracantha is a prickly beauty with stiff, spiny branches that tear and scratch. For that reason it's best espaliered against a wall or grown as a hedge. No one—man or beast—would dare push through its thorny armor! When I cut the branches for bouquets, I slip on my heaviest gloves and proceed with caution. But winter wouldn't be as colorful without its Technicolor touch. For the most abundant bounty, I recommend 'Teton' with yellow-red fruits, or for redder berries, 'Fiery Cascade'.

A Berry Merry Touch

Thinking about pyracantha brings to mind **Skimmia japonica** and its bright fire engine red berries that delight without thorns. It isn't well-known, but it should be. This one is a shade-loving evergreen from the Far East. I recently planted about a dozen along the driveway in front of a clump of Korean silver fir, and I couldn't be more pleased. The low rounded bushes boast dark, glossy green leaves and bear reddish pink buds that open up in April to creamy flowers with the sweetest of scents. Although the female plants produce smaller, less fragrant blooms than the males, they take star billing in winter with flamboyant bunches of bright red berries. One male is needed to pollinate every six females. Since the berries have a bitter taste and are poisonous to boot (a large helping could cause cardiac arrest), the birds don't like them and neither do the deer. **Reeves skimmia (Skimmia reevesiana)** is self-pollinating and lower growing, and not nearly as berried as *S. japonica*. But both its male flowers, pretty in pink, and its dull red fruit appear on the bush together in winter, so it is attention-grabbing all season long.

Golden foliage warms up the garden, especially

A Bamboo in Name Only

Heavenly bamboo (*Nandina* spp.) certainly delivers needed color to my woodland garden. It has clusters of crimson berries, hard and bright and positively cheery against the bamboolike deep green leaves. They seem to be taunting Old Man Winter with their lively appearance, as if to say, "You can't keep us down!" And indeed he can't. The birds don't take the berries, so they stay all winter. They look fabulous in Christmas decorations and mixed into flower arrangements. They can even be kept from year to year, although their color fades.

This evergreen shrub, part of the barberry family and not related to bamboo at all, is a real winner, not a runner. It thrives in sun or shade, with multiple stems that can reach 6 feet or more.

Two dwarf cultivars are worth noting. *N. domestica* 'Harbor Dwarf', a compact cultivar, rounded like an ottoman, displays its brilliant scarlet purple foliage when it is really needed in fall and winter. By summer it is a soft green—a chameleon plant. It stays under 3 feet tall. In spring, it displays panicles of small white flowers; in fall,

on cold, dark days. It lets the sunshine in.

it produces berries and its leaves turn reddish purple.

'Wood's Dwarf' rarely, if ever, flowers or fruits—and I don't care. In fall it dresses up like a punk rocker in loud shades of red, orange, lime, purple, and amber that keep the garden dancing through the winter. I planted a group as groundcovers between the conifers along the driveway. Their feathery quality and short stature also make them good bets for foundation plants, particularly effective in front of large rhodies or azaleas. (See photo on page 61.)

A Berried Clan

Crimson berries are a bonus of **cotoneaster,** a large genus of shrubs, both evergreen and deciduous, that come in a wide range of shapes and sizes with dark green foliage. I've done my dabbling with the low growers since they're excellent groundcovers, and I like seeing the bright berries peep through a dusting of snow as if they were playing hide and seek. What's more, it's easy to tuck bulbs between the fishbone-patterned branches, so just when the birds start pecking at the berries, the bulbs poke through and the transition from winter to spring is even more beautiful.

I like seeing the bright berries peep through a dusting of snow as if playing hide and seek.

Another thing I appreciate about these shrubs is their spreading habit; they can meander over stones, tumble down a bank, or softly edge a walk with their small boxwoodlike foliage. The deciduous cultivars include *C. horizontalis* var. *perpusillus*, only 12 inches tall with an abundance of berries and an evergreen form, and 'Variegatus', under 2 feet tall with a 7-foot spread, its leaves lined in white. *C. dammeri* 'Streib's Findling' is a 6-inch evergreen creeper with tiny white flowers that become vivid red berries in autumn—a perfect backdrop to the earliest bulbs.

Technicolor Leaves

When I mention the shrub **leucothoe** (fetterbush), most people give me a blank look, yet once I point it out, they nod in recognition. It's very popular with landscapers and often used as a foundation plant because it thrives in shade and has an attractive round shape. But best of all, its arching branches support bronzed maroon leaves throughout the winter. A couple of cultivars put on a really gaudy show. *Leucothoe fontanesiana*

OPPOSITE: Cotoneaster scrambles along the ground creating a bright covering for winter.

'**Rainbow**' has striking red stems with colorful mottled foliage, tie-dyed to be exact, sporting pink, cream, green, and copper splotches. '**Scarletta**' is a chameleon with glossy scarlet leaves in spring, dark green in summer, and burgundy in fall and winter.

The Well-Loved Mountain Laurel

One of our most cherished shrubs here in the Northeast, **mountain laurel (*Kalmia* spp.)** has glossy evergreen leaves and gorgeous clusters of pink, red, or white flowers in spring. While many reach 7 to 10 feet high, certain cultivars are more diminutive, making them ideal for small gardens. These little ones are especially effective grouped together, a cheery hit of green in a drab brown landscape. One of the most popular of these petite beauties is *K. latifolia* 'Carol'. The shiny green foliage with wavy margins grows into a dense, low mound. Another species, *K. myrtifolia*, grows more slowly and produces smaller leaves. 'Olympic Wedding' is outstanding because its foliage takes on a maroon tint in winter.

The Overlooked Osmanthus

This holly look-alike is usually grown for its tiny, powerfully fragrant white flowers that appear in fall, but I appreciate it for its shiny, spiny evergreen foliage. An easy way to tell an osmanthus from a holly is to notice the configuration of its leaves. Holly leaves are alternate, while osmanthus leaves grow in pairs along the stem.

Osmanthus makes a superb border plant and even in the toughest of winters, the deer won't nibble it. The only species that is hardy in Zone 7 is *O. heterophyllus,* and a few of its cultivars have especially lovely leaves. 'Purpureus' is a dark beauty with purplish green winter foliage and brighter purple spring growth; 'Variegatus' bears leaves bordered in cream; the foliage of 'Goshiki' is speckled with five colors—pink, green, yellow, gold, and bronze. It is a compact plant, growing to about 6 feet.

The Best of the Boxwood

This small-leaved evergreen deserves a quick mention because the large shrubs are excellent as hedges and the small ones are perfect for edging. **Common boxwood (*Buxus sempervirens*)** is always a winner, with some of the most compelling cultivars bearing leaves touched with yellow. 'Latifolia Maculata' presents foliage with random splotches of gold on a medium shrub; 'Elegantissima' forms a compact dome with tiny, rather misshapen leaves rimmed in creamy silver. It looks great standing alone or as a hedge.

OPPOSITE, CLOCKWISE FROM TOP LEFT: *Nandina* 'Wood's Dwarf'; *Leucothoe axillaris; Osmanthus* 'Goshiki'; *Leucothoe fontanesiana* 'Scarletta'

61

WHAT LIES UNDERFOOT: GROUNDCOVERS FOR WINTER

When the grass has decayed into a depressing brown, you can always depend on evergreen groundcovers to perk up a yard. They truly defy the weather and many can be picked from under the snow to bring indoors for foliage or flower arrangements. Best known are myrtle (**Vinca minor**) and pachysandras (**Pachysandra spp.**), the garden's bread and butter. They are always dependable when I need greens for a flower arrangement or centerpiece. Besides the common varieties seen in all the best places, there are interesting characters that are fun to collect. Allegheny Mountain spurge (*P. procumbens)* is a slow spreader with matte gray-green leaves that have a mottled rather than even coloring. Seek out some variegated pachysandra such as 'Silver Edge' for variety. Among the unusual myrtles, 'Alba Aureavariegata' has yellow-edged leaves and 'Sterling Silver' has glittery white edges. But others that are somewhat less familiar are equally reliable.

Lilyturf (*Liriope* spp.) has dark green, grasslike foliage, plain or striped with silver or gold, about 12 inches high. The plants form tight little tufts and hold their leaves well into winter. By early March, they may look a little scruffy, but so do I when I'm pelted by snow and ice. After a trim, lilyturf quickly grows back. *L. majestic* 'Majestic' has spikes of lilac flowers in fall, followed by black berries that persist through the cold amid green leaves. The skinny blades of *L. muscari* 'Pee Dee Gold Ingot' emerge a strong yellow but eventually mature to a stunning chartreuse and remain that way all winter. It's superb rimming a path.

The leaves of **English ivies (*Hedera helix*)** come in all sorts of shapes, from fans to diamonds, circles to hearts, irregular lobes to tiny birds' feet. Surfaces are smooth, ruffled, wavy, or curled, and sizes can be as tiny as a dime or as large as a salad plate. 'Buttercup' is a golden variety, 'Glacier' has snow white variegation, and 'Goldheart' offers a splash of yellow in the center of the leaves. In winter, 'Goldheart' has a burgundy blush around the gold and the stems are bright red. Any of these look terrific trailing along the ground, but they're also superb scampering over fences or stone walls.

Wintercreeper (*Euonymus fortunei*) is an evergreen vine that forms a closely woven mat. 'Gracilis' has cream and green variegated foliage that blushes in cold weather. I have it climbing a deciduous tree, a winter wrap that puts more color at eye level. I also like 'Kewnsis' because some of the dark green leaves change to red in winter, creating a stunning pattern play. 'Sunspot', 'Moonshadow', and 'Variegata' are yellow-leaved cultivars well worth planting.

OPPOSITE: Wintercreeper 'Gracilis' is equally beautiful climbing a tree or covering the ground.

***Gaultheria procumbens* 'Wintergreen'** has more common names than any plant I've come across. I've counted 34. They range from checkerberry to dewberry, roxberry to pigeonberry and grouseberry. From these latter names I can only assume that wildlife loves wintergreen. Yet I know it can be extremely toxic if ingested by humans. It is the source of wintergreen oil. Clink is another name, completely beyond my understanding, but ground holly makes perfect sense. The evergreen shrublet, as one garden writer described it, looks like holly—that is, if holly was a creeper only 6 inches high. It has beautiful glossy green leaves and plump red berries that release an aroma if rubbed. This native American plant is at home along the East Coast from Georgia to Newfoundland. So why isn't it in more gardens? It is even lovely when its white nodding flowers bloom in summer.

***Arum italicum* 'Pictum'** is a strange one, its behavior the opposite of most plants. It shows up in September, stays through the winter, shows off its berries in spring, then naps the rest of the year. The narrow, arrow-shaped leaves are beautiful glossy green with silver veining and often a purple glow along their edges. The flower is a spathe (sheath) with a skunky smell if you bend over and put your nose in it. It disappears by winter and is followed in spring with bright reddish orange stout clusters of berries that stay for weeks. The mature leaves are wonderfully decorative for indoor arrangements, but the new leaves wilt quickly. This plant is easy to divide and can be planted amid another groundcover, creeping phlox, or euonymus, so it doesn't leave a blank spot when it naps in late spring.

Hens and chicks, such as *Sempervivum tectorum*, blush burgundy in the cold air. They add spots of color and interest in the cracks of our stone walls. 'Royal Rudy' is burgundy year-round. Planted in the ground, they do need perfect drainage. I have heavy clay soil, so besides planting them in my stone walls, I've planted them at the edge of my gravel driveway and in all-weather containers. With their quirky shapes, they have a style all their own. *Sedum spurium* is a mat-forming evergreen species, with saw-toothed green leaves and red stems. 'Elizabeth Red Carpet' only grows to 3 or 4 inches high but with a 2-foot spread. The foliage is dark red with a greenish tinge. 'Dragon's Blood', a sibling, has deep purple foliage. *S. rupestre* 'Angelina' is another spreader, but its leaves are needle-shaped—in fact, from a distance, it resembles a prostrate spruce, with entangled branches. Its luscious lime color is an attention getter wherever you may put it.

The herb **thyme (*Thymus* spp.)** is perfect for placing between paving stones or covering a bank; its tiny leaves form a thick, fragrant evergreen mat. Wooly thyme (*T. pseudonlanuginosus*), so-called because its stems have long fuzzy hairs, makes a tidy silver carpet that turns reddish in winter. The leaves of *T. vulgaris* 'Silver Edge' are outlined in white and in cold weather they sparkle with a hint of rose. I use both between the stepping-stones in our courtyard garden where they fill the cracks and spill over onto the stone.

OPPOSITE: 'Goldheart' ivy blushes in winter with red stems and pink cheeks.

Deciduous Shrubs That Dazzle

It's amazing how the sight of a few brave blossoms under a desolate sky can warm the soul better than the coziest muffler. Even in deepest winter, when flowers are most often found at the florist, there are some shrubs that do put on a show. Yes, their numbers are limited, but I'll take what I can get.

OPPOSITE: The red berries on a mature, deciduous holly add a burst of color to a winter landscape even when dusted in snow.

Over the years I've planted different ones, and although I wish I had more varieties to choose from, I now know what works. I plant the winners in places where I will see them every day out a window or as I drive away when the weather is frightening and I need cheering up.

Generally shrubs that are picturesque in winter are pleasing in the other seasons as well. Many are handsome enough to merit positions as showstoppers, planted singly where they have room to grow to full size without competition. Even if they only flower for 2 or 3 weeks, their berries could be long lasting for a few months or more. If their foliage is attractive and they have high color in fall, they're four-season headliners.

The ones I mention in this chapter are versatile and functional. They act as windbreaks, form hedges, hide unsightly foundations, or anchor a flower border.

WINTER'S BRIGHTEST BLOSSOMERS

If I ruled the world, I'd decree that every homeowner take out a 3-foot-diameter plug of grass and plant a winter-flowering shrub. What a difference it would make in the beauty of our communities and our collective happiness! When we would look out the window or walk down the block, all our senses would have the euphoria of liftoff. Flowers do that, especially those unexpectedly blooming in late winter. And before that when their buds are plump, there is the added pleasure of cutting some branches to force into earlier bloom indoors. Cutting and forcing branches is a good way to keep connected to the winter garden.

Mellow Yellow Flowers

On a gray February day when I open the front door and glimpse **witch hazels'** orange and yellow tassels dangling from bare branches, I know we're blessed. The fiery colors of the wispy four-petaled, spidery flowers blaze against the snow and seem to be daring the weather to put out their fire. There are several varieties in the genus *Hamamelis* that bloom as far north as Zone 5. The earlier-blooming American witch hazels grow up to 10 feet tall and tend to hold their crinkled and dull khaki leaves, making it harder to see the flowers. The Chinese witch hazels and their hybrids slowly grow up to 20 feet and color up beautifully before dropping their leaves in fall. It is a glorious sight as each oval green leaf becomes feathered with red, orange, and yellow like the plumage of an exotic bird.

OPPOSITE: Witch hazels can be cut and brought indoors for winter flower arrangements. Their sweet scent will perfume a room.

AUTUMN EFFORTS

Fall is a good time for planting shrubs because the weather is cool and the newly planted shrubs won't be stressed by high heat. Before planting, ask yourself where a colorful shrub would improve your view. Then choose a plant that will grow to a mature size and shape suitable to your site. Bargains usually are available now. Nurseries don't want to carry a large number of potted shrubs over the winter, so check around to see if what you want is what they don't want. Just be sure to make your purchase before the ground freezes.

But the hybrid *Hamamelis × intermedia* **'Arnold's Promise',** the first that I planted, remains one of my favorites. There's a clump on the lawn that faces the house, and the golden flowers, reminiscent of confetti left dangling after a party, have an endearing disheveled look. I like to pull on my boots and walk outside to inhale their sweet, slightly medicinal scent (think of the astringent made from the shrub) and snip some of the blooms to bring inside.

Other varieties in this species offer different flower colors—bronze, red, amber, pale yellow—and grouping several together produces a display that brightens even the bleakest day. 'Diane' for instance bears crimson blooms, while 'Jelena' sparkles in a brilliant copper and 'Vesna' flaunts her flowers in look-at-me orange with a flush of red.

Happily, witch hazel has a cousin that's just as pretty and fragrant but blooms slightly later. Her name is **winter hazel (Corylopsis),** and she wears many faces. Buttercup witch hazel (*Corylopsis pauciflora*) is a delicate ingénue with dense 1½-inch drooping clusters of buttercup yellow bells suspended freely along her arching bare branches. Refined and rather ethereal, this blooming shrub looks like something the fairies set out and is especially arresting planted en masse with blue scilla at its feet. The small, serrated, light green, heart-shaped leaves follow the flowers and often emerge tinged with pink and amber tones. It is a compact shrub eventually growing to 4 to 6 feet high as far north as Zone 6. It fits nicely into a shady spot where it doesn't draw much attention to itself until late winter when it shines. I have trained summer-blooming clematis to trail over my four shrubs to give them another season of bloom.

Much more theatrical is spike witch hazel *(C. spicata)*. This 4- to 6-foot-tall stunner slowly spreads to about 10 feet wide and drips with 2- to 6-inch-long pendants of bold yellow blooms. The purpley red anthers that embellish its perfumed flower chains add a welcome splash of color in a winter scene that's mostly gray.

But the *Corylopsis* that has captivated me most is a cross between these two. Named 'Winterthur', I saw it first at the Du Pont estate of the same name in Dela-

One of the best witch hazels is 'Arnold's Promise'. It drops all its leaves in late fall and blooms early in winter, holding its flowers for many weeks to spite the weather. OPPOSITE: Winter hazel's drooping clusters of soft yellow bells are not easily damaged when decorated by snow.

ware and it was breathtaking. The original specimen, planted 25 years ago, is now 12 feet high, but most of these shrubs top out at 6 or 7 feet. The fragrant flowers grow in dense panicles and look spectacular against a backdrop of conifers.

Cornelian cherry (*Cornus mas*) can be trained to grow into a small tree 20 to 25 feet high as far north as Zone 4. Or, if left to its own devices, it will stay as a broadly rounded shrub often suckering profusely. Its blooms overlap with the witch hazel, lasting 3 weeks or more, but they are much more refined. The cherry's bare branches are laden with tiny yellow blooms in conspicuous clusters. The flowers form on the previous season's growth. I like to prune it and shape it when it's in flower so I can enjoy the bouquets indoors. Red berries, like small cherries, make an appearance in early fall but they don't stay long once the birds have found them. If I was quicker, I could turn the berries into preserves. The foliage lights up the fall as it turns yellow, orange, or red. Strangely, the leaf color varies from tree to tree and also from year to year. It dances to its own drummer. But the best part is that it is easy to grow in sun or partial shade, easily adapting to most soils.

Holly grapes (*Mahonia japonica*) (sometimes listed as *M. bealei*, since the two are hard to tell apart) is another lemon yellow flowered shrub that struts its stuff in wintertime as far north as Zone 6. Belonging to the barberry family, it also has sharply toothed leaves. I have several Oregon holly grapes (*M. aquifolium*), which are slightly hardier to Zone 5. Like the January specials at department stores, I can always count on them to start the year off right: Even if the musky-scented yellow flowers aren't blooming quite yet, their color shows in their tight buds. I cut off a few short stems with their clusters of flowers and bring them inside for forcing. Once they feel a little heat, the buds burst into bloom and spritz their musky scent. Each cluster has its own bouquet. As for its outdoor appeal, this shrub packs quite a wallop. The clusters of flowers are so thick that they can be seen from several yards away. Their lily-of-the-valley scent is a traveler and catches me by surprise when I'm approaching. Indoors the delicious perfume is a wonderful winter pick-me-up. 'Atropurpurea' has red purple leaves in autumn that green up come summer.

Hybrids that do well in the southern Zones 8 and 9 are 'Buckland' and 'Charity' of *Mahonia × media*. They have particularly long flower spikes—about 16 inches. What a standout in somber gray surroundings! Wouldn't you know it, 'Charity' has notable offspring—'Hope' is a bright yellow and 'Faith' a softer color.

When the holly grape's flowers are finished, luscious clusters of purple or black berries follow and decorate the shrub for months. Perfumed flowers, decorative fruits,

LET THE SUNSHINE IN

It's a mystery why so many winter-blooming shrubs bear yellow flowers. One theory goes that pollinating insects are attracted to the color of the sun, so when there's little sunshine in the sky up above, they flock to whatever is on the ground that mimics it.

attractive foliage—holly grape is a shrub that provides interest all year round.

Winter jasmine (*Jasminum nudiflorum*) is somewhere between a shrub and a vine. In the South it grows up and over arbors. At my house after a dozen years, its loose-limbed branches arch up, over, and back down to the ground. In the North it reaches from 3 to 4 feet high and 4 to 7 feet wide; whereas in the South, 15 feet high is more like it if it is trained to grow up a wall or over a trellis. I can't be bothered to make it climb, having to peg it up as it grows, so I think of it as a fountain of yellow flowers especially when it blooms in late winter. The arching stems are lined from top to bottom with red buds that open into 1-inch yellow trumpets. They are lovely in flower arrangements but regrettably lack the scent their family is known for. I can prune the plants and force the branches indoors to my heart's delight without reducing the number of flowers on the plant the next year. Both old and new wood are covered in blooms. Cuttings also readily root and the plants thrive even in poor soils.

Oregon holly grapes hold their yellow buds until the end of winter when they finally open. However, they can be easily forced to open if some of their stems are cut and brought inside. Their wonderful perfume is one of winter's treats.

A Sure Pick-Me-Up

Of course, the so-called "Empress of Winter"—the elegant **camellia**—would seem an obvious choice for winter impact since it is hardy to my Zone 7, but it's been a disappointment in my neck of the woods. I planted a dozen about 20 years ago but only a few are left—and I swear they only exist to taunt me. They always flower, but usually briefly. Mother Nature plays her game and drops the temperature below freezing, and I am greeted the next morning by ugly, withered blooms. Even if I pick them as soon as they open, once I bring them indoors, they quickly shatter in a day or two. Not surprisingly, the survivors are tucked into a rather sheltered area.

I remind myself that although camellias are renowned for their winter bloom, they do best in what is called the "camellia belt" (an area from northern Washington, DC, down along the Atlantic and Gulf coasts into Texas and up along the Pacific to coastal British Columbia). Their gorgeous blossoms bloom as early as January on evergreen shrubs or small trees 12 to 15 feet tall. They prefer moist soil in semishade with shelter from cold drying winds.

I thought I'd have to cross this one off my winter list until recently, when I was told about some new varieties bred to be hardier. The list includes the mid- and late-blooming *Camellia japonica* 'Kumasaka' and 'Rev. John Drayton', both pink; 'Dixie Knight' and 'Governor Mouton', both red; and 'Purity', a sparkling white. They're worth a try.

Something New to Try

As any gardener will tell you, we gardeners are gamblers at heart, not afraid to place a bet on a new plant. That's why I always leave the garden gate open, in hopes that another beauty finds its way in.

I'm going to scout out a little-known but very intriguing shrub **spiketail (*Stachyurus praecox*),** which is hardy in Zones 7 to 10. I saw it recently in a garden at the end of Long Island and was captivated by its long drooping chains of small, pale yellow blossoms swaying on bare mahogany stems. The flowers are produced at each leaf bud and bloom before the plant leafs out. From a distance, all that was visible were the flower necklaces, rows and rows of them, cascading in graceful swags. Eye candy indeed, but I soon learned this beauty plays hard to get; although it's exhibited in botanical gardens and prized by private collectors, it's not available at most nurseries. Luckily, some mail order catalogs carry it.

When winter shrubs bloom, spring is at the starting gate. The marathon of spring bloomers picks up the pace. And passing along the flowering torch, the overlapping blooms of star magnolia, Chinese redbud, white and yellow forsythia, honeysuckle, quince, broom, kerria, daphne, and lilac race on, propelling us into the faster changing landscape.

OPPOSITE: A camellia is the "Empress of Winter" in southern gardens. It is not happy to be covered in snow in my Zone 7 garden. Although it won't kill the shrub, snow often damages the fragile flowers. Consequently, it is best grown in southern states.

The orange berries of *Ilex verticillata* 'Aurantiaca' are a colorful addition to the winter garden and brighten an indoor bouquet or even a Christmas wreath.

FRUITS AND BERRIES

The sight of bright berries dotting a winter landscape inevitably brightens the view. Berries also feed the birds, and a flock of gluttonous birds gobbling the berries is a show in itself—entertainment for the whole family. Even if you're not a fan of birds, the plumage of cardinals and blue jays makes you look. A woodpecker reminds me of an abstract painting in black and white with one perfectly placed red splash. Occasionally, a pheasant wanders into our yard and once a neighbor's peacock did. Now that's a show!

Of course, every shrub that has fruit in winter must flower, so if the shrub is beautiful in winter, be assured it is also spectacular in other seasons. The ones I mention here are year-round beauties.

Winterberry (*Ilex verticillata*) is hardy to Zone 3 and doesn't mind poorly drained sites like mine. It is a holly cousin and well worth inviting in. Unlike its relative, winterberry drops its leaves in winter so its luscious red fruits take pride of place. The only problem is that the birds crave the berries as much as I do. One year I draped black netting over a few bushes to encourage our fine-feathered friends to look elsewhere for dinner. Unfortunately, a bird found its way in but couldn't get back out. It gorged itself until I pulled the netting off. Now I only pray that the birds leave some berries to glow against the snow. As a precaution, I cut some branches early to use inside for Christmas decorations.

At Landcraft Nursery on Long Island last winter, the birds denuded a huge clump of winterberry by mid-December. It was unusual. They often last all winter, but we had a summer drought and the birds didn't have plentiful pickings. The opposite problem was evident at the Morris Arboretum in Philadelphia, where the director Paul Meyer noted when I visited his garden in March that he was tired of looking at the masses of berries and wondered why the birds hadn't claimed them. Every year is different.

I've also heard that the birds steer clear of yellow berries until late winter when their choices are few, so I'll have to add *I. verticillata* 'Sundrops' to my collection.

Ron Solt, president of the Holly Society of America and a friend of mine, recommends *I. verticillata* 'Aurantiaca', an orange-berried cultivar; *I. opaca* 'Morgan's Gold', a primrose yellow holly with a red blush on its cheeks; and 'Christmas Snow', a variegated favorite resembling its name. Of course, the longstalk holly (*I. pedunculosa*) is another favorite, since its berries hang on long stems like cherries. Ron could easily list more favorites, since his passion has taken him all over the world to search out cultivars of holly for his historical collection, now numbering more than 200. There are so many choices: cultivars with large or small, spiny or round, shiny or dull foliage and everything in between. Lively variegated cultivars with green leaves highlighted in gold or silver add to the choices.

Year-Round Appeal

Naughty but nice, **Japanese barberries (*Berberis thunbergii*)** have red berries that last all winter on severely thorny stems, so plant them away from any path. I planted a few for all the wrong reasons. I wanted to shield my fragile roses from our basketball court, so I planted a couple of barberries as a barrier to keep the ball on the court.

In Ron Solt's garden, two deciduous hollies, 'Winter Red' and 'Aurantiaca', bounce their bright colors off of each other. Together they provide a welcome pick-me-up on gray winter days.

My hope was that my sons and their friends would think twice about sending balls their way in order to avoid the thorns. But boys will be boys and they didn't give a lick about the thorns—each scratch was a badge of courage. However, in the process, I came to appreciate a shrub I might never have planted otherwise. It is truly a four-season delight: red-tinged yellow flowers in spring; striking leaves in summer in all sorts of shades, from the deep burgundy of *B. thunbergii atropurpurea* to the sprightly gold of *B. thunbergii* 'Aurea'; scarlet foliage in fall; and glistening red pendants of oval berries that cling through the winter and attract birds as well as grateful glances from me. 'Crimson Pygmy' is a compact dwarf that grows less than 2 feet tall. All barberries make great hedges, since they are very dense and can be sheared a few times a year. They prefer full sun and well-drained soil, but they can grow in sand and do tolerate drought. They grow up to Zone 4.

Berries of Another Color

Much less dangerous but equally striking is **beauty berry (*Callicarpa*)** that grows as far north as Zone 6. The small white flowers lining its stems are not much to talk about, but once the plush purple berries appear, the shrub is not to be missed. Beauty berry is a medium-size ornamental shrub that drops its leaves after the first frost to reveal stunning lavender berries that hold on through the winter months. The color is so startling that people who see the shrub for the first time can't help but gasp. It is just as striking in flower arrangements or Christmas wreaths.

One of the best beauty berries is *Callicarpa bodinieri* var. *giraldii* 'Profusion', 8 feet tall with cascading branches. In fall, its oval leaves take on a marvelous mauve tone, beautiful against its amethyst fruit. It's gorgeous grouped with other callicarpas as a backdrop for a border or in a cluster. Although I'm partial to the color purple, there are selections that offer white berries. A good choice for Zones 8 to 10 is *C. japonica* 'Leucocarpa', a rounded bush that grows about 5 feet by 5 feet, with big bunches of berries. Like others, it produces maximum fruit when planted with more than one species or cultivar close by.

A caveat: Although beauty berry fruit can last most of the winter, I have a hard time keeping the birds away. So I was surprised and delighted when the birds hadn't found the beauty bush at my friend Ron Solt's garden in Pennsylvania. Its berry-laden branches were prime for cutting. How did he do it? I asked. His explanation was that the bush was protected by trees and shrubs growing nearby. It wasn't in the open where it would act like a neon sign for birds. Short of draping netting, which is tricky since birds sometimes find their way underneath, this idea of a screen of other shrubs seems to be a good solution.

OPPOSITE: 'Crimson Pygmy' barberry's thorny stems look harmless when covered with snow, but don't risk pruning it without wearing gloves.

No-Fail Beauty

A plant pro once told me that there are viburnums to suit every garden in every season. And he was right. This vast genus includes more than 225 species, but the ones I'll mention here are those that yield berries or flowers in winter. And in my neck of the woods, that narrows the choices to the following species.

American cranberry bush (*Viburnum trilobum*) is an oldie but goodie. It's been growing here in the United States for centuries, It was cherished by the colonists as far north as Zone 2 for its winter fruit, which was high in vitamin C—sorely needed in those days. While I have yet to make a conserve from the berries, I definitely endorse their picture-perfect prettiness: The translucent scarlet fruits against a backdrop of pristine white snow make you wish you had a camera in hand. 'Wentworth' can reach 12 feet tall by 12 feet wide, but 'Compactum' is a dwarf form (only 6 feet tall) that fruits just as abundantly and looks every bit as striking.

The **linden viburnum (*V. dilatatum*)** is another keeper for New England winters as cold as Zone 6. This beauty grows to a shapely 8 feet tall, with toothed leaves resembling those of linden trees. Tiny white flowers form domes as large as 5 inches across when they bloom in late spring and early summer, followed by oval scarlet berries

The clusters of viburnum berries act like catcher's mitts. They easily hold the snow. OPPOSITE: When *Viburnum* 'Dawn' bloomed in early February, it looked like a miracle had taken place, since everything else was covered in snow.

81

The simple addition of a
bench in front of an evergreen hedge makes a winter
scene more inviting.

83

that stay in place through the winter months. 'Catskill' and 'Iroquois' flaunt red fruit, 'Michael Dodge' offers yellow fruit, and 'Erie' parades a profusion of red berries that fade to pink when the temperature drops.

To get off the subject of berries for a moment—**V. × *bodnantense* 'Dawn'** is a memorable member of the viburnum family that I must mention. In my New York garden, the flower buds appear in February like pink tubular tassels swaying on totally bare stems. Then they wait until the temperature warms or the sun hits them to unfurl and release their sweet perfume. Amazingly, even during a Vermont winter at Joe Eck and Wayne Winterrowd's Zone 4 garden, this hybrid has been known to unfurl a few of its pink blushed blossoms when it gets a whiff of slightly milder weather. Yes, it happens only intermittently, but the fact that it happens at all is utterly amazing. Most shrub books don't recommend growing it above Zone 7.

Out of the Ordinary

Like a gourmand who is always ready to taste something different, I have a couple of other new shrubs to put on the table. The first is **Symphoricarpos,** sometimes called **coralberry or snowberry,** depending on the color of the fruit. These bushy shrubs bear tiny, bell-shaped white flowers in fall, but they're only a prelude to the bountiful berries that appear later. *S. × doorenbosii* 'Magic Berry' delivers loads of rosy fruit that deepen to an eye-catching cranberry color as they mature. *S. × doorenbosii* 'White Hedge' is stunning with large white berries on the tips of its stems as well as along the sides. The berries on both of these Dutch hybrids stand up well to the rigors of winter.

Another one to keep a lookout for is **red chokeberry (*Aronia arbutifolia* 'Brilliantissima').** Don't let the name mislead you; the fruits on these vase-shaped shrubs won't make anyone choke, even the birds, but our winged friends do leave them alone because of their astringent taste. Many chokeberries can reach 10 feet tall as far north as Zone 4, but 'Brilliantissima' is more compact and tends to bear larger berries that grow in clusters.

OPPOSITE: A blue jay looked in our window to thank us after gobbling up our offering of cracked corn hanging on the river birch.

FOR THE BIRDS

Winter color doesn't always stem from flowers, foliage, or berries. Some of the most surprising jolts come from birds. I hang feeders throughout the garden to encourage our fine-feathered friends to visit. I have a 'New Dawn' rose that scrambles up the second story of our house and sprawls over the balcony railing. A wide range of birds stops by to nibble on the rose hips, often staging an original musical. Out the living room window is a holly that is the preferred resting spot for plump blue jays. Yesterday I counted five nestled among its branches, enjoying the view and ignoring the fruit. Perhaps the birds were too sated to fly. And the star magnolia that I see outside my kitchen window has a bird feeder hanging from its lower branches, so there is always a frenzy of activity going on there. I fill it with cracked corn, which has a high oil content and is reputed to help keep the birds warm. The birds eat every scrap of it, and it doesn't leave a mess as the sunflower and other seeds do. The larger birds, cardinals and woodpeckers, intimidate the smaller ones. Occasionally a red hawk swoops in, or a wild turkey or a pheasant strolls up, and that is always a memorable sight.

Very Merry Berries

Almost nothing gives me greater pleasure than foraging outside for branches of berries to bring indoors for arrangements. Even a few small stems nestled into a mint julep cup make a charming winter welcome on a dinner table or on a guest's bedside table. To keep the berries going longer, cut the stems on a slant so they have a larger area to take up more water from.

Beauty berry (*Callicarpa americana*): Harvest when 90 percent of the berries are a true amethyst tone and most of the leaves have fallen. Recut the stems inside, remove remaining leaves, and place the stems in warm water. The fruit often dries on the stem.

Holly (*Ilex opaca*): Harvest anytime. Condition branches by submerging them overnight in water. Then arrange as desired. If using dry, mist daily. Holly should last 2 weeks or more in water.

Winterberry (*Ilex verticillata*): Harvest when the berries are red and the leaves have fallen. Place the stems in warm water, then keep in a cool place until ready to arrange. Freshly picked berries should last for weeks indoors and several months outdoors in cool weather.

Juniper (*Juniperus*): The blue berries are long-lasting even out of water. I always remove some of the foliage around the clusters to expose more berries.

Crab apples (*Malus*): Many crab apples have fruit that stays all winter. Cut twigs of it and recut them on an angle to give them a larger surface to help take up water.

Heavenly bamboo (*Nandina domestica*): The clusters of hard red berries can be harvested anytime, and they will last for years untreated, although their bright color fades from one year to the next.

Firethorn (*Pyracantha*): These are difficult to harvest because of the thorns. Wear heavy gloves when cutting and arranging them.

HIP, HIP, HOORAY

Rose hips are brilliant against a green backdrop. The smaller hips last longer than the fat fleshy ones. The most readily available hips come from multiflora rose, a roadside menace that crowds out our native plants. I have vines of it climbing the trees in our woods. Years ago I tried to get rid of it but the birds drop their seeds and the roots run underground, with new shrubs popping up in other places. Since I can't easily destroy it, I have learned to control it somewhat and to enjoy its fragrant small white once-blooming flowers and collect its hips for bouquets and wreaths. I admit a tangle of them on otherwise all-too-bare canes is an arresting sight in winter.

Rose hips are great holiday perk-me-ups for wreaths, swags, and garlands. I sometimes spray mine with a light coating of matte or shiny shellac to keep their color from fading and to preserve them. Treated this way, they even last from one year to the next. These are my top picks of better-behaved roses that produce good rose hips.

- 'Ballerina'
- 'Belinda'
- 'Blush Noisette'
- 'Cecile Brunner'
- 'The Fairy'
- *Rosa eglanteria*

As festive and as decorative as a holiday wreath, a hanging metal cone is covered with moss, wrapped with ivy, and filled with assorted rose hips, holly, blue spruce, and other greens.

Perennial Pleasures: Perennials and Grasses

Until 2007 ended his record, the groundhog had seen his shadow on February 2, signaling another 6 weeks of winter, for 8 years running. Actually, in 2007, the groundhog was wrong. Winter lasted into the third week of April, far later

OPPOSITE: Dried flowers left in the garden on perennials, annuals, and shrubs add interest to the winter scene. Like this hydrangea bloom, they may even end up as the base for an ice sculpture.

89

than in the other years. To me, that's all the more reason to keep searching for plants to cheer up the landscape. Over the years I've found reliable winners—hellebores, lungworts, primroses, and heaths among them. I'm convinced each year that I'll continue adding to the list. In the process I've discovered the value of grasses. Although they may not actually "bloom" during the winter months, they hold their seed heads' shape and volume and deliver exquisite pattern and texture. Including them in the landscape is a strategy I totally embrace.

WINTER'S PERENNIAL BLOOMERS

It seems impossible that there could be plants that bloom in winter, yet it is so. And there are many. Given such a wonderful gift by Mother Nature, wouldn't you think people everywhere would be so grateful that they would plant them for all to see? It would be a simple thing, but it would make such a difference in the beauty of our surroundings. All of the perennials mentioned here will return year after year once they are planted. None are difficult to grow. So let's set an example by planting some and thus spread the word.

The Miracle of Hellebores

Hellebores (*Helleborus* spp.) are selfless little flowers that bloom when most perennials are sleeping, in colors from bright white to light green to dusty pink, mauve, and plum. The winsome blossoms go nonstop for 3 months or more, starting in mid- to late winter. Different species are called Christmas or Lenten roses because of the time of year they bloom. Most years, mine show their pretty faces in February, but if the weather has been mild, they may greet me sooner. The foliage on all varieties is evergreen—leathery leaves with saw-toothed edges—and the plants spread prolifically. To be blunt, they're totally promiscuous, meeting and greeting and breeding with such abandon that the most frequently available hellebores are now classified as *Helleborus* × *hybridus*. In fact, there are new cultivars introduced all the time with double flowers, bigger blossoms, and more colors. All hellebores are worth trying, and I'd recommend first acquainting yourself with these four species that are easy to grow. Of course, if you want to keep them true to form, plant each species in a separate area.

The **Christmas rose (*H. niger*)** is the first to bloom, a diminutive darling not more than 12 inches high. The 2-inch white flowers lie flat like saucers above foliage divided into seven leaflets. Over time the petals age to lime, but the yellow stamens remain bright and glistening, resembling a nest of golden threads.

OPPOSITE: When this hybrid hellebore first opens, it is quite colorful. As it ages, the pink fades to cream.

It is followed by the **Lenten rose (*H. orientalis*),** with wide-open nodding blossoms in bluish white, mauve, or plum. The 3- to 4-inch flowers are beautifully spotted or blushed inside with crimson, maroon, and green, varying from blossom to blossom and from plant to plant. This is the species I originally bought and the one that dominates my hillside, perhaps because the plants self-sow so readily. Don't panic. They are not walkers. Lots of tiny seedlings sprout under their mother's foliage skirt, and I have to scoop them up and transplant them to spread them to new areas. Their survival rate has been almost 100 percent. Consequently, I carelessly move them whenever I feel like it, even in hot, dry summers. Of course I water them in. Since the plants are so love-crazy, it may be that most of what is now in my garden are *H. × hybridus*, a label that has almost become synonymous with *H. orientalis*.

H. × hybridus is also the label that most mail-order sources use these days. Heronswood Nursery in the Pacific Northwest carries an incredible strain called 'Heronswood Doubles', with blossoms boasting two rows of slightly cupped petals. 'Heronswood Red', another exclusive, presents large outward facing flowers in a luminous red tint.

Bear's foot hellebore (*H. foetidus*) blooms about the same time as the hybrids. It has clusters of hanging, tight-lipped lime green bells, some edged with just a smudge of maroon, suspended about 32 inches above the ground. In cold weather, the leaves turn a glossy dark olive, and the contrast against the chartreuse stalks and flowers is stunning. The Latin name *foetidus* means fetid or foul-smelling, but any unpleasant odor is released only when a leaf is broken or crushed.

Corsican hellebore (*H. argutifolius*) is the big daddy of the bunch, reaching 3 to 4 feet in height. It bears the palest green cups, held well above the foliage, and inside each flower is a tuft of green stamens. The sharply spined leaves are a pale grayish green and unlike those of its cousins, the leaves are all the way up the stem, not just at the base.

Whenever I read the directions for growing hellebores— "Keep evenly moist and never allow them to dry out"—bells go off in my head. A Gunga Din nightmare comes to mind: I'm out morning, noon, and night poking my finger into the soil to see if it is dry, then toting a watering can to keep them "evenly" moist. It's not going to happen! Luckily, it is totally unnecessary. I watch them come through high heat and drought better than the other perennials in my garden.

ZONE IN

When I tired of growing strawberry begonias (*Saxifraga stolonifera*) as houseplants, I planted them outdoors along my woodland path, thinking they would last just one summer since they were only hardy to Zone 8. They have stayed for 10 years, and their scalloped, hairy geranium-like leaves decorate the winter garden with white veining and red undersides. They are not bothered by snow or low temperatures, and I am still amazed at their survival instincts.

So my advice to all gardeners is not to take zone guidelines too seriously. Many plants can successfully live in colder climates than recommended. For whatever reason—a good snow cover, a protected corner, a microclimate, a gardener's green thumb—a certain specimen may prove the zone map wrong. Some plants have not been adequately tested, and there are so many variables it's impossible to be exact. So while I wouldn't suggest putting a Zone 8 plant in a Zone 5 site, try jumping one zone colder. Place your choice plant in a protected site, cross your fingers, and you may be lucky.

OPPOSITE: The colors in *Hellebores* x *hybridus* vary greatly. CLOCKWISE FROM TOP LEFT: A close-up of a hybrid hellebore; a mixture of hellebores collected to bring indoors; a close-up of another hybrid hellebore shows the wide variations in color from seedlings; at the base of the mother plant dozens of seedlings have sprouted.

93

"Resents disturbance" is another crazy idea that is oft repeated in books. If that is so, how did hellebores ever get moved into so many gardens? Why have I never lost one when I scoop up the babies and transplant them to new spots? I'm glad I didn't read how to care for them before I planted them. I've been moving them around for years, and my soil often dries out in summer. In fact, they have survived one summer's drought without problems.

A close-up of the heath *Erica carnea* 'December Red' in bloom
OPPOSITE: In our carriage yard, the early daffodils bloom with the heather. The perennials are just emerging.

The Quiet Beauty of Heaths

Often confused with heather, which blooms in summer and fall, **heaths (*Erica* spp.)** are a boon for winter gardeners. Why they are so overlooked is a mystery, because the small but showy blossoms make their entrance just as other blooms have exited. These ground-hugging shrubs have very fine foliage, and flower spikes that appear in bunches at the tips of the stems and continue blooming for months. Although they tolerate some shade, the best color is achieved in full sun and well-drained, acid soil. Since heaths are relatively small, no more than 18 inches high, they're best placed in rock gardens or at the edge of a border. I've planted some at the bottom of a retaining wall in a garden built on top of a gravel driveway, where the drainage is perfect, and also between stones in our courtyard. Their perky flowers spill over the stones, demanding attention from anyone nearby.

E. carnea is a hardy species that spreads into low carpets of needlelike leaves. 'December Red' lives up to its name by producing rosy pink blooms at the end of the year. Better yet, the flowers stay on through late spring. 'Golden Starlet' has sunny gold foliage and sparkling white flowers. Then there's 'Springwood Pink', a well-known cultivar with pale pink flowers that are ideal for cutting.

E. × *darleyensis* is bushier in habit with leaves that frequently go bronze in winter. I'm partial to the deep lilac flowers of 'Furzey', a real pleaser with beautiful foliage that starts off a pinky red. The long-blooming 'Kramer's Rote' always coaxes a smile from me with its magenta blossoms and bronzy purple winter leaves.

Primroses

There are many species of **primroses (*Primula* spp.)** that hold their foliage all winter and even throw up the occasional bloom before their all-out spring celebration. Primroses are snugglers, too, and unite one perennial to another. They edge a hill-side of hellebores at my house as well as many paths. Their colors shout that spring is on its way in red, orange, yellow, blue, purple, white, and any other color you like. They also bloom in bright combinations—navy and yellow, scarlet and cream, orange and white.

If you plant an assortment of different species, you can have primroses in bloom into May. Each species starts and ends at a different time. Happily *P. polyanthus*, a petite 6- to 10-inch charmer, often blooms quite early and stays 6 weeks or more. I sometimes spy a gaily colored blossom nestled close to its leaves in my woodland garden in late January or February if there is a stretch of mild weather. These plants take it in their stride if they are snowed upon when they are beginning to flower. They won't bloom full out, lifting their blossoms above the foliage, until they believe they've left snow and ice behind.

Some unusual cultivars recently have been introduced, such as 'Penumbra', a silver-laced form named for the edge of light seen around the moon during an eclipse. The flowers' centers are bright yellow and borders are dark mahogany rimmed in silver. One of our yellow hose-in-hose primroses from the *Primula tomasinii* 'You and Me' series bore a small flower last January, but that's not normal. The hose-in-hose primroses that I have usually bloom a few weeks after the polyanthus start. *P. veris*,

the English cowslip primrose, is a late-winter, early-spring bloomer that keeps going full-out for 6 weeks or more, sending up clusters of sweetly scented nodding bells. Their stems are 6 to 8 inches long, making them easy to cut and enjoy indoors.

Lungworts

In a shady spot in my woodland garden, I have had flowers nodding from small **lungworts (Pulmonaria spp.)** by mid-February. Unlike other perennials that grow their foliage first and then flower, this charmer sends up foliage and flowers together. Almost as soon as I spot the petite leaves aboveground in a clump that only covers a few inches, I can usually find a bud or open flower. As the plant continues to grow for the next few months, it continues to produce flowers. When it stops blooming in May, the plant has increased its size several times. By summer's end, the leaves are at least 5 inches long. Thank goodness, because this deciduous perennial is known as much for its foliage as for its fetching flowers.

Indeed, the white spotted leaves of *P. saccharata* 'Mrs. Moon' resemble swatches of polka-dotted fabric, and they always demand a second glance. The blossoms—funnel-shaped and borne on clusters on 10- to 12-inch stems—are equally intriguing: The flowers start off pink then turn to blue. How do they do that? I like them best when there is a mixture of blue and pink flowers. *P. angustifolia* 'Azurea' has plain green leaves but the same changing blooms. *P. officinalis* 'Sissinghurst White' is true to its name with pure white blooms.

ABOVE, LEFT TO RIGHT: Yellow English cowslips mingle with forget-me-nots; 'Mrs. Moon' is a speckled lungwort with both pink and blue flowers.
OPPOSITE, LEFT TO RIGHT: A polyanthus primrose's leaves are surrounded by snow; a polyanthus primrose blooms in late winter.

Catch It If You Can

Petasites, also known as butterbur, should only be recommended with reservation. This plant has such strong roots, its foliage is so large, and it travels so fast that it wouldn't surprise me if it picked up a small child on its leaf and carried him about the garden.

I complained vehemently in an e-mail to Wayne Winterrowd who gave me a small root of *Petasites hybridus* years ago. I wasn't sure if he was a friend playing a practical joke—or a foe. Wayne wrote back, "Don't scorn petasites, Suzy, just don't! Of course it is high maintenance, keeping it in bounds. But what is gardening, if we don't work at it? There is no hardy plant quite like it, for its elegance of form and its tropical appearance, well into Zone 4. I would defend it to my death."

Wayne also loves the flowers that bloom before the leaves appear. Minty green cauliflower-like blooms rise up before the heart-shaped foliage, almost 3 feet across, appears at the end of winter on *Petasites hybridus*. The flower dome is a rosette of daisy-like discs held up on thick foot-high stalks.

Collecting hellebores and petasites flowers for an indoor arrangement is one of winter's pleasures. OPPOSITE: The smiley yellow faces of spring adonis brighten a shady spot under a deciduous tree.

On *Petasites japonicus*, the flower stalk stretches up and matures with muddy pink blooms along the top, most appropriate as mud season follows closely behind its bloom time. The umbrella-like leaves follow the flowers and quickly grow as if on steroids to 3 to 4 feet across. It's an odd character to be sure, but attention-getting in a bouquet.

I have large clumps of both growing at the bottom of a slope where the garden ends and the beach begins. Some charge up the hill, and I regularly pull them up. I've lifted a yard-long fat rope of running root, yanking it up a foot at a time as I followed its course, before it broke off. Digging it up is great for working out angst. Perhaps confining it in tubs would be the answer for those who want it without the worry that it will take over their gardens.

Spring Adonis

Rarely seen but easy to grow, **adonis (_Adonis amurensis_),** also known as pheasant's eye, reminds me of calendula and dandelions—perhaps not its best selling point. But nevertheless, there it is, and I actually love them all. Well, maybe I love dandelions best since they are so easy to care for and long-blooming. Nothing embroiders a lawn like they do, except maybe the earliest bulbs and _Veronica repens._

Back to adonis: It's a lovely little thing that is best suited to colder climates, but it will grow in Zones 3 to 9. It grows about 15 inches high with finely cut foliage and 2-inch buttercup yellow flowers, fully packed with 20 to 50 petals. A feat at any time of year! 'Flore-plena' is the showiest one, a double that could bloom for 6 weeks alongside the crocus and dwarf iris if the weather is cool. The plant grows from rhizomes and is slow to spread. It has to be mass planted from the get-go or it won't make much of a statement. By summer adonis is dormant, so it should be grown next to a late riser—balloon flowers are a possibility and annuals another.

A. vernalis blooms 3 to 6 weeks later and is hardy to Zone 3 with protection.

BEAUTY IN THE EYE OF THE BEHOLDER

Adonis flowers are similar in appearance to dandelions. Why are they coveted and dandelions not? Who made this distinction so long ago, and why do most gardeners believe it? Why is a lawn so sacred we can't have flowers blooming in it? Lawns are so boring. Visitors find it quite shocking to find dandelions in full bloom in my lawn along with the daffodils and crocuses. I actually grow them quite well. And since I don't use chemicals on the lawn nor do I plan to weed it anytime soon, there they'll stay. I usually explain to visitors that I don't have a lawn at all but a close-cropped meadow. That's my story and I'm sticking to it.

Even the golden tresses of *Hakonechloa* 'Aureola' bleach out in winter but its short bob holds its shape and never needs a haircut. OPPOSITE: *Miscanthus sinensis* shimmers in the breeze and sparkles when dusted with snow.

SPLENDOR IN THE GRASS

Henry James may have proclaimed that there are no sweeter words in the English language than "summer afternoon," but he wasn't watching the way ornamental grasses glisten when frosted and dusted with snow. The cold emphasizes the translucency of the foliage and the seed heads, and as the blades bend in the wind, they seem to clasp the rays of the sun and lead the rays in a sparkling dance. Most grasses also retain their volume, so they fill space in the often-empty winter garden. Add to this the spectacle of birds coming and going to enjoy the shelter and seeds, and the value of ornamental grass increases.

When working with grasses, try to place them where they will catch the early morning or late afternoon sunshine. And put them in a spot that welcomes breezes. Personally, I'm not as fond of them in a flower border where their movement is restricted. This usually means choosing an unsheltered site, smack in the middle of the lawn perhaps, or one near a tunnel of trees or shrubs that directs the air forward. Mine are at the far end of our pond just off the bay. As the moving air coaxes the stems to sway, streams of golden light shine over the all-too-dull landscape.

Grasses can also be a major design feature. A large solo clump can act as a living sculpture while a parade of several types can create a hedge. Arching grasses soften a hardscape instantly, moving the eye upward and bringing it right back down. Shorter varieties, planted in sweeps, mimic a meadow. And both the tall and the short can work wonders in the winter providing much needed texture and form.

Gardeners Prefer Blondes

Most grasses turn blonde in the winter. But, like hair color, all blondes are not the same. Some are rich almond, some pale champagne, others warm butterscotch. And when the rays hit these various tones of gold, it seems as if the sun is sitting right there in the garden. The blondes on my list include the following:

Japanese variegated silver grass (*Miscanthus sinensis* 'Variegatus') never looks better than when its color has been turned caramel by repeated frosts. This clump-forming

plant has reedlike stems and narrow arching leaves that can reach 6 feet high with a spread just as wide. Feathery plumes debut in late summer and persist till frost. The lovely sepia color is a particularly beautiful backdrop for early-blooming bulbs.

Fountain grass (*Pennisetum alopercuroides*) is a 3- to 4-foot-tall beauty with graceful arching foliage that dries to a golden tan. The soft bottlebrush seed heads have a radiant copper glow and persist well into the winter months. A fleeting hoarfrost or dusting of snow turns them into frilly confections of spun sugar and twinkling diamonds.

Switch grass 'Heavy Metal' (*Panicum virgatum* 'Heavy Metal') gets its name from the striking blue gray color of its 4- to 5-foot skinny leaves, which are a knockout in the summer garden. Once a heavy frost occurs, however, the blades bleach out, turning to an ashy platinum that remains attractive all winter long.

Named the Perennial Plant of the Year in 2001, ***Calamagrostis* × *acutiflora* 'Karl Foerster'** sports 2- to 3-foot deep green foliage that shakes and shimmies in the slightest breeze. The 5-foot plumes of creamy flowers make a splendid show in summer and are followed by golden seed heads. Leave these on until a heavy snowfall knocks them down or cut them for intriguing additions to winter arrangements.

Beyond Blonde

Fescue seldom blooms but when it does, it has straw-colored flower heads. The spiky blue blades of fescue arch like the tousled hair on a punk rocker and hold their color all winter. Most species form dense clumps 1 foot wide and 1 foot tall. *Festuca glauca* 'Boulder Blue' is an intense azure that's a bit smaller than the species, while 'Elijah Blue' is a powdery blue shade and even shorter.

The thin arching pale blue leaves of **blue oat grass (*Helictotrichon sempervirens*)** are imposing even without its blue summer flowers. It's terrific alone as an accent or in small groups.

Sedge (*Carex*) is easily confused with true grasses. This vast genus is known for its grasslike, clump-forming foliage that ranges in height from 1 to 3½ feet tall. *C. flagellifera* 'Kiwi' has skinny, cascading leaves in a tempting shade of lime; *C. siderostica* 'Variegata' displays broader leaves, green with a white margin. For a sedge of a different color, there's *C. flacca* 'Blue Zinger', with wide pleated leaves that usually retain their blue gray color through the frosty months.

Ribbon grass (*Phalaris arundinacea*) is a striped grass that thrives in boggy sites and is a vigorous grower—in fact, sometimes it can be invasive. But the bold banding on the 2- to 3-foot blades makes it a knockout. *P. arundinacea* 'Strawberries and Cream' has skinny green and white blades that blush with pink during winter.

OPPOSITE: When capped with snow, the seed heads of *Miscanthus sinensis* are arresting. A clump of grass can have the weight and beauty of a living sculpture in the landscape.

ADDED ATTRACTIONS: DRIED FLOWERS AND SEED HEADS

Come autumn, I used to shear all my perennials, pull up the annuals, and mulch the borders. Then it dawned on me that too tidy a cleanup leaves a garden without character—dull and boring. Now I leave the ones that stand tall even after their life retreats into their roots. Stiff and strong, many dried stalks and flower heads withstand pelting snow and ice with a most sober bearing while others show the crooked spine of age.

Flowers, seed heads, and foliage that dry naturally add texture, interest, and height to the garden. Ornamental grasses, hydrangeas, or black-eyed Susans add an assortment of sturdy browns to early winter and become showy shapes.

Many pods are quite dramatic, and letting them be encourages self-seeding. Rosalind Creasy, a great gardener and garden writer, said, "Our tidiness crowds out nature. In some climates hummingbird mothers collect Japanese anemone's 'fluff,' soft as cotton balls, for their nests—very comfy." The "fluff" appears when the seed pod opens, carrying seeds on the wind to new places.

Of course, I can get into trouble leaving prolific seeders like **perilla,** although their honey brown stems and seeds are attractive. I leave **black-eyed Susan**'s "eyes" to peer at the landscape all winter. Consequently, their clumps get slightly fatter each summer. Frost really works its magic on coneflower's domed seed heads, transforming them into huge diamond stickpins. The silvery elliptical pods of poppies look like something dropped from a spaceship, and they come in a variety of sizes. The 5-foot-tall stems of **Veronica longifolia** with their spiky spires remind me of a Giacometti sculpture.

The big fat flower heads of **Sedum 'Autumn Joy'** are a garden's chameleon, changing colors with the seasons. Its silver foliage flaunts green flower heads in July, pink in August, reddish in September, and deep brown in winter. Each stem stands 2 feet tall, waiting to be capped with snow.

Astilbe refuses to spread by seed but the feathery skeleton of its flower remains to add substance to the garden. The feathery flowers dry to a soft reddish brown that melds exceedingly well with winter's monochromatic scheme. Coated with snow, sea lavender's dried flower sprays resemble underwater plants from *Finding Nemo.*

WATCH OUT FOR FLYING SEEDS

To shade their porch from the summer sun, Dennis Schrader and his partner Bill Smith built a trellis. Now their porch is a favorite place for entertaining when the weather allows. Dennis planted a wisteria to grow up the trellis, and it is decorative all year. In spring fragrant blooms dangle from the green foliage; in summer, it's a restful green roof; in fall, it's bright yellow with large brown seedpods hanging down; and in winter the seedpods ripen and usually burst open when the sun hits them on a warm February day. Dennis says, "It sounds like machine-gun fire as the seeds go flying about, hitting the window and sides of the house. The pods then spiral up like corkscrews. I never would have noticed if the wisteria wasn't by the front door."

The bottlebrush spikes of **Cimicifuga** dim to a pale taupe, but they still retain their theatrical allure. The **honesty plant (Lunaria annua)** isn't called silver dollar plant for nothing; its flat, round, silvery pods are even more lovely with a sprinkling of snow.

St. John's wort and **liriope** in a mild winter might be evergreen; more often I need to shear them back in late winter. **Hydrangea's** dried flower heads act as catcher's mitts, grabbing and holding snowballs. Mop-head cultivars bleach to a warm tan and hold their petals until they are clipped off in early spring. The lace-cap types look like antique lace.

With the first frosty sheen, everything glimmers and takes on a new majesty. **Hosta** flower stems ripen and brown with nodding open bells—a great shape for holiday gilding. The foliage of hosta bleaches white and shrivels like sheets of papers blown about, so I toss them on the compost pile.

Even the vegetable garden takes on its own personality if plants are left standing. **Sunflowers** are a favorite food of birds. A friendly family of giant, 6-foot sunflowers bending over to sow their seed is a humorous sight. Sometimes when I walk the nearby path and see them out of the corner of my eye, I think someone is watching me. And someone is! It's the ghost of gardens past.

Wisteria seedpods ripen in winter when the sun warms them, then burst open, spitting seeds all about.

Snowflakes

Scientists know snowflakes are not frozen raindrops. They are crystals of ice that grow out of the water vapor in the air, tiny clouds that freeze as they drift down to earth. The whole process of making a snowflake takes about 15 minutes, and each is unique. Even the smallest flake, no larger than the head of a pin, has its own pattern. Different temperatures and wind conditions produce the various patterns. Needlelike and columnar designs dominate in warmer conditions, while star-shaped designs gather when the temperatures are lower. But scientists can only surmise how the water molecules change into dramatically diverse crystal structures. How a snowflake is formed is baffling.

Dr. Kenneth Libbrecht, head of the physics department at Caltech, explains, "No other substance grows in such a fascinating variety of crystalline forms as ice. Depending on weather conditions, snowflakes can grow into slender needles, thick columns, thin plates, multibranched stars, or countless other intriguing shapes."

Using a photo-microscope, Dr. Libbrecht examines and photographs snowflakes in all of their various forms. He has discovered that flakes with six nearly symmetrical arms are common, but flakes with 12 arms have been photographed as well. Strangely, snowflakes never have eight sides or points.

In a light snowfall when the temperature is low and there is little wind to distort them, elaborately designed flakes glide to earth. This is the time to catch some on the sleeve of your coat and grab a magnifying glass to examine them. Lucky for us, it is easy to see the individuality and beauty of snowflakes with even a dime-store magnifying glass. It is a wonderful activity to introduce children to the wonders of nature.

For more details and beautiful pictures of snowflakes, read *The Snowflake*, *Winter's Secret Beauty*, by Dr. Kenneth Libbrecht (Voyageur Press, 2003).

OPPOSITE: These photographs of snowflakes were taken by Dr. Kenneth Libbrecht using a photo-microscope. It is only a sampling of their many beautiful guises since no two are alike. For more pictures and information, visit www.SnowCrystals.com.

Labor of Love

The smallest gift often makes the biggest impact. Just ask Kay Macy. She would never have guessed that the how-to booklet on drying flowers her husband gave her more than 50 years ago would have led to her life's work. Henry Macy liked to joke that the booklet that started his wife's career was the best investment he ever made.

Over the past 50 years, Kay has perfected the art of drying flowers. Her flowers look fresh from the garden. "I have a house full of flowers in the middle of winter," she says. "It doesn't get much better than that." Surprisingly, her dried flowers hold their vibrant colors and perfect shapes—it is often difficult to tell that they are dried.

Preserving flowers is a year-round activity for Kay. She plants and grows a wide assortment of flowers and harvests most of them as they near their peak. Dahlias are picked when they have already reached their peak. Distinctions like this are crucial for drying perfect flowers.

Picking starts in April with daffodils. Kay picks first thing in the morning, after the dew has burned off. Moisture on the petals leads to decay. Some flowers such as dahlias are picked on short stems to avoid cutting off any unopened buds growing lower on the same stem. A short flower stem is easily lengthened by wiring it onto a dried stem of *Verbena bonariarensis,* which reseeds so readily around Kay's garden.

Each flower is preserved immediately after picking. Everlastings, strawflowers, yarrow, hydrangea, *Artemisia* 'Silver Queen', nigella seedpods, and celosia dry naturally. Kay hangs them in a dry, dark closet where the humidity is kept below 60 percent. Each type of flower is hung upside down in small bundles held together by rubber bands. The weight of the flower heads holds the stems straight for the weeks it takes for them to completely dry. Most other flowers, including ageratum, roses, tulips, delphinium, larkspur, and salvia, are preserved by burying them in a shoe box filled with silica gel. Silica gel is a granular, moisture-absorbing chemical that slowly, over a few days or a week, draws the water out of the flowers and even out of the air. The silica can be reused over and over again if it is dried out in a low-temperature oven.

Most books say dahlias do not dry well, but that didn't stop Kay. Dahlias are her pride and joy. She grows more than 70 different varieties. "Such an enormous array of color and shadings, and they hold up so well," she says. She places a few inches of the gel in the bottom of a shoe box and gently lays each dahlia on top. Her trick is to use a small scoop to nudge silica gel into every fold and under every petal. Each petal has to be dried properly so it will hold up the petal on top of it.

Tulips are difficult, too, but she discovered that if each one is placed in a paper cup slightly larger than the bloom, the cup holds the petals upright as the silica gel is added. They dry easily and hold their shape.

Each box is dated, then checked often over the next week to determine when the flowers are ready to remove from the gel. If they are still moist, they'll be limp and won't hold their shape; if they are too dry, they'll be brittle and the petals will fall off. Once properly dried, the flowers are arranged by colors and laid on screens or poked into moisture-resistant florist foam in a windowless room with low humidity. Here they stay until fall, when Kay is ready to arrange them.

Late fall and winter she spends happily arranging her dried flowers. This is when the artist in her takes over. She mixes flowers from different seasons into romantic, voluptuous, and colorful arrangements to deliver to her customers. Daffodils mingle with roses and dahlias as in the bouquets of 18th-century painters. The fragile flowers are best arranged so they don't overlap or touch, so the arrangements are airy enough for bees to fly through them.

One arrangement I purchased lasted for 3 years, because it was placed on a table in a

windowless hallway of my husband's office. The hall was heated in the winter and air-conditioned in the summer, so its temperature stayed constant. The bouquet was not touched by sunlight, so the flowers didn't fade. Visitors always thought the flowers were fresh.

Word of mouth has spread the news about Kay's stunningly beautiful bouquets. They have been showcased in all the best places, such as the Metropolitan Museum of Art's American wing, Tiffany & Co., and private homes.

An arrangement of Kay's dried flowers includes her favorite dahlias, delphinium, tulips, nigella, and inkberry foliage.
OPPOSITE: Kay Macy at home in her studio

Early-Blooming Bulbs

A gardener teamed with a bold imagination and a strong back can easily turn a winter landscape into a paradise. Actually, forget the strong back: Early-blooming bulbs, as small as buttons, slip into the soil without much effort at all.

OPPOSITE: The earliest bloomers in the winter garden include dwarf iris, snow crocus, and winter aconite. They take snow and ice in stride.

Consequently, I plant more of them each fall to hasten the scent and splendor of spring. Snowdrops, winter aconite, crocus, scilla—I can poke hundreds into a loamy bed in less than an hour. Mass planting intensifies the impact. Even if I covered all the gardens and buttonholed the lawn with bulbs, I would always find room for more. Early bulbs (I'm lumping in corms and tubers as well since they behave in much the same way) are dependable, forgiving, lovable, and cheerful. They cost little, yet they increase in numbers and beauty each year—a bargain to be sure. So why don't we see them everywhere? Is it because of the myth that you need a cast-iron back to plant them?

Once the bulbs are planted, I never know when they will appear. Forget the calendar! Each year they show up in a different week, depending on the amount of snowfall and the temperatures. But that's what makes them all the more endearing. What a happy surprise to walk to the car one morning along a walkway newly frilled with flowers. Or to rinse out your coffee cup, bleary-eyed, and spy a sunny band of *Eranthis* from the kitchen window.

A WHIFF OF FLORAL PERFUME

Many winter bulbs waft entrancing, if gentle, aromas. Outside in the cold air, they tend to be shy, hugging the earth and holding fast their sweet breath. But once indoors, the warmer temperature releases their perfume. Snowdrops, winter aconite, and snow crocus in particular make beguiling bouquets. I like to tuck them into teacups or juice glasses at each place setting to cheer up a winter dinner. Guests are always charmed, and doubly so when they realize these nosegays were plucked from the garden just hours before.

Later bloomers—dwarf iris, assorted daffodils, and tulips—also offer scented flowers. So to make your bulb growing twice as nice, check to see which species and cultivars are scented before placing your orders.

OPPOSITE: The golden globes of winter aconite bloom above fringed green collars. Their sunny appearance is in sharp contrast to their icy bed.

MAKE ROOM

The diminutive size of these blooms means they must be planted where they're easily seen. However, since they flower when most trees and shrubs are naked and the perennials have not yet shown up, opportunities abound. Snowdrops, crocuses, glory-of-the-snow, and scilla are lovely planted into a lawn. Their leaves wither soon after the petals drop so mowing is not delayed. A crowd of early bulbs under a tree or between foundation plantings is another unexpected pleasure. Puschkinia cozying up to a bare lilac or scilla romping among a trio of hydrangea is a most welcome sight. I originally planted them on the outskirts and together they seeded in all the gaps. It is surprising how happy they are snuggling against the shrubs' stems. Some of the flowers use the lilac trunks as backrests. I massed a group of early bloomers under an ornamental weeping cherry on the front lawn. Three seasons of the year, the foliage is so dense that it makes a perfect hiding place for children. To make it an official "enchanted room" in summer, I did a little pruning to open a door, added a child-size arbor, and placed kid-size furniture inside. Now, when the bulbs bloom in February or March, visitors are fascinated by the fairyland of tiny blossoms viewed through the weeping curtain of branches.

THE CULT OF THE SNOWDROP

Altogether there are 23 *Galanthus* species and hundreds of cultivars, each with its own distinguishing traits, although I admit I only recognize a few. But bands of Galanthrophiles (snowdrop cultists) can point out discreet differences just like that. They tell me that the shades of green on the blossoms can vary from bright apple to dull sage, that the foliage might be narrow or wide, curly or straight, and that the perfume can be strong or mild. So dedicated are these fans that they scout out antique, naturalized drifts and search on bended knee for new treasures. Or they invest in the more unusual ones, paying perhaps $10 to $100 for a single bulb. Indeed, by acquiring these uncommon specimens, it is possible to have snowdrops in flower from October to March. Some that collectors covet are 'Walrus', with two tusklike petals; 'Lady Elphinstone', a double with yellow markings; and 'Wendy's Gold', a single yellow. 'Sam Arnott' has larger flowers and heart-shape green markings, perfect for Valentine's Day.

Regardless of the depth of your devotion—or your pocketbook—no one should be without snowdrops. Even if you have some already, plant some more. There is plenty of room for experimentation and new combinations to keep your interest going. Temple Nursery in Trumanburg, New York, ships unusual snowdrops "in the green" in April. Buying "in the green," while the bulbs are actively growing in soil, almost always guarantees success if you plant them out as soon as they arrive. However, you don't need to be in the grip of collecting mania to enjoy a patch of snowdrops; commonly available cultivars are bargains in fall.

Rarely seen, but wonderful to behold, is a tapestry of bulbs fluttering over a dozing flower bed. Large numbers of a few species do the trick, creating an intriguing interlude between seasons. And they can be placed anywhere in a border, even at the very back because during the winter months, nothing blocks the view. Just take a look at your property on a winter day and decide where some color would be most welcome. That's where the bulbs should go.

Enter the Three Stooges

Snowdrops, winter aconite, and crocus are the garden's equivalent of the Three Stooges. Knocked down, pelted, and frequently wearing silly hats of ice and snow, they stand up again and again, never knowing what hit them. It is slapstick comedy, garden-style. And I get giddy with delight just watching.

Snowdrops (*Galanthus* spp.), usually the first of these comedians to put on a show, announce winter is waning by ringing their creamy bells. Their miraculous return year after year is illustrated by the bank of blooms leading down to the beach at my house. I can take no credit for these fearless flowers—they were planted more than 80 years ago and keep spreading! The fact that they colonize so vigorously, undeterred by snow and ice, is proof that the common snowdrop (*G. nivalis*) can be set in the soil and simply forgotten.

'Flore Pleno' is a frilly, double-flowered cultivar with irregular, crisp white outer petals surrounding an inner rosette striped with light green. True doubles don't reseed but they do multiply. I help mine along every few years by splitting up the clumps during a thaw and replanting them immediately. Or, I may pot up a bunch—doubles or singles—and bring them inside for a well-deserved vacation. When the flowers are spent, I simply plant the clump outside in a new spot, knowing there's a good chance I may have jump-started a whole new colony.

I've also planted the giant snowdrop (*G. elwesii*) with bells twice the size of its well-known sister. Unfortunately, it's slow to naturalize up here in the North; this bulb is better behaved in the South. But no matter. I appreciate the fact that it's a bit

taller (about 10 inches high), the leaves are wider, and the green-tipped blossoms are just that much bigger.

Sometimes blooming neck and neck with the snowdrops, although often closely behind, is **winter aconite (*Eranthis hyemalis*),** our second stooge. This heirloom from 1570 has lemon buttercup-like flowers standing above a furled green collar. From a distance, even on the grayest day, a clump glows as if the sun's rays had dropped to Earth. *E. cilicica* is similar but bears deeply divided bronze foliage when it first appears; its leaves change to green before the sunny yellow globes arrive.

Planting winter aconite in large numbers is the key to establishing large colonies. Put them in shady spots, but steer away from the lawn itself because the foliage hangs around for months and should not be mowed down. And take a tip from one who has been down the garden path: Soak the corms in water overnight before you put them in the ground. At the time they're sold in fall, they're quite shriveled and need some plumping up to prepare for their best show in late winter.

A wise way to produce dazzling drifts of flowers is to dig up mature clumps and move them while they are actively growing. This process of transplanting—called "in the green"—increases the odds of a spectacular display (for more, see page 128). Supposedly, winter aconite prefers a limey soil, but at my place, it thrives under tulip poplars in decidedly acid earth.

A young colony takes a few years to take hold but then little seedlings continue to pop up, more each year. They start with a pair of small leaves one spring, then sport a ruff of foliage the next winter, and finally the golden flower heads rest atop the foliage ruffle. It's a slow but sure affair and eventually the colony naturalizes, taking over a larger and larger area.

Our third stooge, the well-loved **crocus (*Crocus* spp.),** typically shows its colors as the snowdrops and winter aconite are closing up. During the winter season, the wineglass-shaped flowers bloom in many colors—blue, purple, yellow, white, orange, red, and bicolors—like scattered gemstones sparkling on the ground. The earliest blooming varieties, those that do their thing December into January, are costumed like Las Vegas showgirls. Take *C. sieberi* 'Tricolor' for instance: She's a brazen hussy gussied up in lilac, white, and gold. *C. imperati* wears buff feathers outside, with lavender and purple inside. And when she yawns, she exposes an orange stigma and a yellow throat. *C. biflorus* 'Miss Vain' fits right in with her snowy white petals with pale blue bottoms and neon

FRUGAL GARDENERS, LISTEN UP

Bulbs are the biggest bargain in the garden world. Spend $20 for a few hundred tiny nuggets, devote a couple of hours to planting, and you will have weeks of enjoyment for years to come. Becky Heath, a co-owner of Brent and Becky's Bulbs, says, "We have seen a hundred crocuses become thousands over the course of several years. If an assortment of crocuses is planted out in a meadow or a lawn, they are likely to crossbreed, and the self-sown results could be quite beautiful and unique."

Think of bulbs as socks and shoes. For as Becky puts it, "They fill in around the naked ankles of larger plants," making the overall effect "so much better."

orange streaks. And wouldn't you know it, she is heavily perfumed to boot.

If I could grow only one crocus, it would be the February-blooming snow crocus (*C. chrysanthus*). But then why would I only grow one? This stunner, though, always captures my heart with its flush of bright petals poking up through the snow. Although it's not more than 5 inches tall, the species is noteworthy for its unusual color blends, not found in the larger hybrids. It makes the most dramatic appearance when planted in clumps of one color and blooms so profusely and so brightly that even small clusters can be seen from a distance. *C. chrysanthus* 'Goldlilocks' is as intense a yellow as its name suggests, while 'Advance' is a fetching blend of violet bronze and butter with a straw interior. (*Note:* In the South, these bulbs bloom in late January.)

Another winning crocus is *C. tommasinianus*, which blooms somewhat later, usually in mid- to late March here on Long Island. I'm partial to this species because it is especially dependable and long-lived, among the best for naturalizing. What's more, it's the least likely to be dug up by squirrels, the crocus's number-one enemy. So every year I put in more cultivars like 'Ruby Giant', a spectacular violet, and 'Barr's Purple', a splendid amethyst. But just in case, as with all my crocuses, I spread a sheet of chicken wire over my newly planted bulbs, making sure it extends a few inches in each direction, peg it down with wire hairpins, and hide it with mulch. So far my primitive remedy has worked; the rodents have been too lazy to dig in sideways. Once the bulbs have started to sprout, I remove the screen.

A Blues Quartet

Nothing is prettier in wintertime than the appearance of blue flowers; they're a promise of blue skies and warmer weather ahead. Happily, there are three bulbs that deliver that needed dose of azure on even the bleakest days.

Glory-of-the-snow (*Chionodoxa luciliae* syn. *C. gigantea*), another March bloomer at my place, has heavenly blue flowers with white-starred faces. They twinkle on a frosty day with eight to ten blossoms facing upward in a cluster. The foliage is light green and unobtrusive, disappearing quickly after the flowers bloom. 'Alba' has white petals and 'Gigantea' is a larger blue form. *C. forbesii* is an heirloom variety with rich blue blooms; 'Pink Giant' is large with only a light pink tint. Plant these babies in large colonies under deciduous trees or mixed into a low-growing groundcover.

Blue puschkinia (*Puschkinia scilloides*) is trouble-free and inexpensive and is a charmer with its delicate coloring, each petal the faded blue of denim with a darker blue central strip. So why is it not more often planted? It is puzzling indeed.

Puschkinia is a hardy soul, withstanding any weather but hail and high heat. It has a singular habit of blooming the moment the fully formed bud pushes through the ground. If the weather is not to its liking, the fragrant, half-inch blooms lay their heads on the ground and wait until it is. Then the stems shoot up with 6 to 12 bells lining each stem almost the whole way from top to bottom. The foliage matures quickly after the flowers have faded, so this is a good bulb to plant into a lawn. But no matter where it is planted, it will happily colonize.

However, Puschkinia's colonies pale next to *Scilla siberica*. This bulb has turned my hillside into a sea of blue in 20 years. Whether you call it scilla, squill, wood squill, or one of its other aliases, it is a very memorable bulb when planted in masses. I recommend it highly. Unlike most of its early-blooming brethren, its delicate blue flowers thrive in low light and are particularly pretty tucked under evergreen shrubs or outlining a shady border. *S. siberica* 'Spring Beauty' is a bigger, better cultivar than the species and has intense blue blossoms dangling from 6-inch stems. In fact, it has become so popular, people often think 'Spring Beauty' is the common name of the bulb. But no matter, this charmer's jaunty skip through the garden delights me anew each spring and when my hillside blooms, it matches the blue of the sky.

Most scillas—and there are many to choose from—overlap with the snowdrops and stay to greet the earliest daffs. They're prized for their naturalizing capabilities and their ribbonlike foliage matures quickly, making them an excellent choice for studding the lawn. I'm partial to *S. tubergeniana* for two reasons: It shows up even sooner than 'Spring Beauty', in early March, and its blue pinstripes on palest blue petals are totally beguiling. Who could resist?

Perhaps the bluest of these blues comes from **grape hyacinths (*Muscari* spp.),** a group

OPPOSITE: *Scilla siberica* is one of the great naturalizers, turning our hillside into a sea of blue with islands of daffodil clumps. Neither bulb crowds the other out.

A close-up of an *Iris reticulata* bloom shows the details of its wonderfully colorful markings.

of bulbs that blooms from March till May, depending on the variety. Fantastic naturalizers, they throw off successive spikes of what look like tiny upside-down grapes for weeks on end. While they like sun, grape hyacinths can take some shade and tolerate most any soil. One of the earliest to flower is *M. armeniacum* 'Christmas Pearl', a 6-inch stunner in a violet blue that's utterly captivating. Just as precocious is *M. azureum* with brilliant tufts of electric blue blooms on 8- to 10-inch stems. Both are perfect partners for early-blooming daffodils.

Petite Charmers

Joining the promenade of late-winter bloomers are **rock garden irises,** sometimes referred to as dwarf irises. These gently perfumed cuties may be short (the stems are only 4 inches) but their theatrical 2-inch headdresses never go unnoticed. The inner petals, called *standards*, pose upright, while the outer ones, called *falls*, open downward to reveal a contrasting splotch of color. I tuck these irises along walkways and in the crannies between paving stones where they seem to leap up out of nowhere to greet me. *Iris danfordiae* is a delicious yellow with deeper yellow falls spotted with green. The multi-flowering *I. bucharica* steps out with creamy standards and pale lemon falls speckled with gold. If blues and purples are more to your liking, *I. reticulata* fills the bill. 'Pixie' is dark blue, almost black, 'Harmony' has sky blue flowers with yellow streaks, and 'Natascha' is a bluish white with green veining and a golden blotch. *I. reticulata* often comes as a mixture of varieties—a good way to get acquainted with these little darlings. Try planting a dozen per square foot for impact.

Elizabeth Lawrence, a southern garden writer, thought it a wonder that *Iris unguicularis* ever showed its face, embarrassed by its ugly name. But these bulbs, often called Algerian or winter iris, are beautiful little things, varying in color from the pale lavender of 'Walter Butt' to the deep violet blue of 'Marginata'. Living in Zone 7, I've been able to grow them, but gardeners in colder zones may have to resort to potting them up. Which is not all bad, because as author and plantswoman Pamela Harper states: "Brought indoors, they open up so quickly that one can watch the buds unfurl, a live time-lapse performance enhanced by the sweet scent of newly opened flowers."

A clump of dwarf iris blooms under the branches of a deciduous shrub.

Winter Windfalls

Hardy cyclamen (*Cyclamen coum*) look like a miniature version of the familiar holiday plants sold at nurseries and florists. Like those of its hothouse cousin, its dark green leaves are heart-shaped and marbled with silver, and its flowers boast floppy petals in shades of pink, red, and white—but they are only about 1 inch across on 3-inch stems.

Since the plants are small, I've placed several on top of a stone wall where I can easily see them against a background of juniper. They're a glorious sight, bursting into bloom in November and sending up more stems that flower over a 6-week period. (Sometimes they'll flower again in early spring.) Despite cold and nasty weather, the cyclamens will jauntily wave their blossoms, beckoning visitors to give them a friendly stroke or two. I've read that if left for many years, the round tubers could grow to the size of a hockey puck with hundreds of blooms. Wouldn't that be something!

Cyclamen tubers must be planted concave side up, $\frac{1}{2}$ inch deep, in rich, well-drained soil and in a place protected from harsh fall winds, rains, and snow. They resent drying out and will not tolerate any layering of plants on top of them, even though they are summer snoozers. Roots grow from the top of the tuber as well as the bottom, so be very careful when digging around them. Although slow to multiply, cyclamen tubers prefer to be left undisturbed in a snug spot. One of my decade-old clumps has slowly crawled under an evergreen shrub and is quite content. A deep snow cover helps it survive and should not be removed.

New Versions of Old Favorites

Wordsworth immortalized the **narcissus** with his words "a host of golden daffodils," but he was probably talking about spring bloomers. Lucky for us, there are a few members of this large and gifted family that actually toss their pretty heads somewhat sooner. Indeed, if well planned, a naturalized daffodil planting, including early, mid- and late-season bloomers, could last 2 to 3 months or longer depending on winter weather.

Daffodils are more than just pretty faces. They are poisonous and inedible to most animals, deer included. In California, they are "critter control" under fruit trees. They keep out gophers.

My choices for some winter magic begin with *Narcissus asturiensis*. This tiny plant, only 4 inches tall, is a perfect miniature of a yellow trumpet daffodil. It usually blooms the third week of February in my Zone 7 garden—a forerunner of spring to come. And even though 'February Gold' doesn't live up to its name—it usually appears mid-March—I wouldn't trade the large colony in my woodland for anything.

OPPOSITE: The open white-starred blue faces of glory-of-the-snow shine up at the golden trumpets of early daffs. The combination is perfect since each brings out the best in the other.

Its sulfur yellow blossoms light up the path like miniature lanterns. I've regularly dug up a few clumps and planted them somewhere else to colonize.

Other early bloomers include 'Tete-a-tete', 'Trevithian', and 'Peeping Tom', easily identified for his large snoot. Like 'February Gold', they are all part of a group called Cyclamineus Narcissi, so named because their petals curve backward, much like cyclamen. All are very durable, naturalize easily, and force beautifully. 'Jenny' is another goodie, an ice queen with a pale primrose cup that matures to pure white.

One of the more unusual daffodils, *N. bulbocodium conspicuus*, often called Yellow Hoop Petticoat, is named for its funnel-shaped flower that resembles an old-fashioned skirt. Recently, botanists dropped the narcissus from its name, moving the bulb into its own genus, but most bulb sellers haven't gotten around to making the change. *N. bulbocodium* 'Golden Bells' is 8 inches tall, twice as tall as the species, and each bulb sends up 5 to 15 blossoms. The flowers, blooming early to midseason, measure only 1 inch long and a few inches high. Because of their distinct shape, they make a superb show along the edges of my woodland path, and their narrow, rushlike foliage stays all winter.

Along with daffs, **tulips (*Tulipa* spp.)** are the most popular bulbs, but most of them

Cyclamens jauntily wave their blossoms,

are latecomers, waiting until May or June to make an appearance. However, there are some advance runners called species tulips. Ancestors of today's hybrids, these often perennialize and are ideal for rock gardens. One of these is *T. humilis violacea*, sometimes called the red crocus tulip. Although only about 5 inches high, there's nothing shy about this lady: She's done up in a wonderful purple-rose color with a yellow base and lime anthers. A close cousin with a name that's a mouthful is *T. humilis alba coerulea oculata*. This variety is glistening white, but a steely blue base makes her a real attention-getter.

A few other favorites are the peppermint-stick tulip (*T. clusiana*), *T. tarda*, and *T. turkestanica*. *T. clusiana* is one of the oldest in cultivation, dating to 1606 or earlier. If you plant it, it's going to stick around. As its name implies, its white petals are striped with cheery red lines atop 14-inch stems. *T. tarda*, on the other hand, is short, just 3 inches high, but its flamboyant clusters of yellow and white star flowers open almost flat, so it is very showy. *T. turkestanica*, the earliest of this trio, is star-shaped with white petals and an orangey bottom.

Daffodils and hellebores are flattened by snow but both will rise again when the sun warms them.
OPPOSITE, LEFT TO RIGHT: 'February Gold' daffodils are one of the first to appear; the small 'Tete-a-tete' daffodils make more of an impact blooming in a birdbath where they are easily seen. More are planted in the ground at its base.

beckoning visitors to give them a friendly stroke.

THE ART OF NATURALIZING

How closely together you plant your bulbs is a matter of taste. Do you prefer to see the distinct shapes of individual plants or do you like the casual overlapping of flowers and foliage? Since I admire gardens where blooms intermingle and stems lean on each other for support, I plant my bulbs at least a third closer than bulb growers recommend. I'm just too impatient to sit back and wait years until the bulbs have multiplied enough to hide the bare soil!

Essentially what I do is imitate what happens in nature. Instead of lining up the bulbs in straight lines like soldiers in a parade, I plant mine in free-form groups.

There are two traditional methods of accomplishing this: Plant them as if they rolled out of a basket and scattered across the lawn, or imitate a stream that widens here, narrows there, as it lazily meanders between trees and around shrubs.

Most bulbs can be naturalized into a groundcover—such as ivy, pachysandra, vinca, ajuga, or liriope—or into a lawn with equal success, as long as the bulbs are tall enough to be seen above the covers. The only advantage of planting in a groundcover rather than in the lawn is that you don't have to worry about mowing if the type of bulb you planted—daffodils are one—takes its time departing. The leaves of all bulbs have to be allowed to die back on their own before they are removed, or there will be no blooms the following year.

LAYER IT ON

Since you're digging the holes anyway, why not pack in some later bloomers with the early bloomers? Prepare a hole 10 inches deep, about the width and circumference of a dinner plate. In the bottom of the hole, place 2 inches of well-drained compost-enriched soil. Place one crown imperial (*Fritillaria imperialis*) in the center of this, or a lily if you prefer, and surround it with six daffodils, equally spaced on top of the soil. Cover with soil, about 4 inches down from the surface. Place a dozen scilla or glory-of-the-snow, or a mix of both equally spaced, in this layer. Completely cover them with 1 inch of soil and add a final tier of a dozen snowdrops, equally spaced. Cover them with soil. Water the area well. The snowdrops will bloom a month or so before the scilla and glory-of-the-snow. An early daff might glimpse the smaller bulbs but a later bloomer arrives after they have departed.

OPPOSITE: The woodland walk in March is beginning its spring show with early daffodils, primroses, and scilla in bloom.

I plant my bulbs at least a third closer than bulb growers recommend. I'm just too impatient to sit back and wait years until the bulbs have multiplied enough to hide the bare soil!

In the Green

Most of us have been fooled into believing fall is the only time for planting bulbs because it is then that they are for sale. On the other hand, many experts believe the right time for dividing and transplanting bulbs is when they are "in the green." If bulbs are transplanted while they are still actively growing and have soil around their bulbs, they don't dry out. I only know of one catalog that sells snowdrops "in the green" in spring, but you can sometimes find them potted in nurseries. Or, if you have friends with a large clump of bloomers, perhaps they will let you dig up a clump. Then again, if you are handy with a flashlight and a trowel and are not afraid of jumping a fence in the middle of the night, you might try your luck at gathering your own.

Most spring bulbs are propagated abroad in Holland and England. Our government requires that bulbs be washed clean of soil before they can be imported to prevent soilborne diseases and insects from entering the country.

In fall, dividing and moving bulbs is an impossible task. A gardener stabs blindly into the general area where spring bulbs have bloomed. Although most bulbs can be left undisturbed indefinitely if they are happily situated, there are three good reasons for digging them up and dividing them. One reason for division is a sparsely blooming clump, a sure sign that they have become overcrowded and the soil is exhausted around them. Another is to speed up their proliferation. Lifting a clump every few years and teasing out individual bulbs before replanting them somehow compounds their rate of natural multiplication.

The third reason is my favorite one: Spring offers another opportunity—or a second chance—to reassess the balance of color in your garden. In early spring, it's great to have an excuse to stay outside. That's why I find digging and dividing bulbs a simple and pleasant chore. After the blooms fade is usually the best time, because there is no danger of damaging the flower.

BASICS ON BULBS

- A rule of thumb is to plant each bulb to a depth of three times its diameter. Once in the ground, bulbs put down roots. As soon as the soil begins to thaw in late winter or spring, bulbs utilize their food reserves to push up their shoots, develop their foliage, and flower. After flowering, the foliage continues to grow. It is during this time that photosynthesis refills the bulbs with food reserves to feed next year's flowers. At the same time, the bulbs set seed, which is one way they propagate themselves.

- The foliage of all bulbs (as well as corms, rhizomes, and tubers) must start to yellow before it is removed or else the bulb will be robbed of its food supply. Conveniently, the foliage of most small bulbs withers quickly and never become a nuisance.

- True bulbs—snowdrops, daffodils, and tulips—also develop buds between their fleshy scales that mature into new bulbs. Corms, on the other hand, annually replace themselves with a new corm or corms that form on top of the exhausted parent once the leaves have died back completely. Tubers simply increase in size and number of blooms.

- Most early-blooming bulbs appreciate a 2- or 3-inch layer of mulch to help moderate soil temperature. The mulch also breaks down over the course of the year and puts nutrients back into the soil. However, don't pile mulch up around the trunk of a tree or shrub; keep it 10 inches away, so mice won't nest there and gnaw at its bark.

Spring offers another opportunity to

Replant with sufficient room for the bulbs to develop. Work humus into the bottom of the hole a few inches deeper than the bulb is planted, to give the bulbs enriched and nutritious soil for their roots to grow into. Water well and allow the foliage to yellow before removing it.

After a decade or so when your bulbs have naturalized and are filling in the spaces between stones in a path or the bare soil under deciduous shrubs, you will have turned your piece of ground into your own little paradise. And for certain you will be wondering why you didn't plant more in the first place. So take it from me—plant bulbs by the buckets, not simply by the dozens.

Early bloomers such as snowdrops and crocus can be dug, divided, and replanted in spring as soon as the soil is warm enough to dig. The bulbs have no problem adjusting to a move when they are in flower. If you wait too long before dividing them, they might have disappeared until the following year.

reassess the balance of color in your garden.

Winter Containers

In this oh-so-quiet season when plants are sleeping and the only garden excitement may be the silhouettes of the fir trees against a cloudy sky, containers step out of their supporting roles and take a star turn. An urn planted with evergreens or conifers and capped with snow is a thing of beauty; the same goes for hanging

OPPOSITE: In Cooperstown, New York, an arrangement of greens, highlighted by the stems of red-twig dogwood, sits on a post at the entrance to a house where it is easily noticed.

baskets and window boxes overflowing with assorted cuttings from conifers, berries, ivy, seed heads, and dried flowers.

I've spent many a happy hour gathering nature's bits and pieces to perk up planters empty of plants. Usually I approach it much like Christmas decorating and remix the same ingredients from around the garden, this time keeping them outside and simply poking them into moist soil or floral foam in pots, window boxes, and hanging baskets.

BOUGHS AND BERRIES

I resort to tried-and-true tricks to fill up many of the all-weather containers that sit in the garden year-round. Otherwise, the empty pots make winter all the more gloomy. I snip a mixture of greens and berry-strewn branches and simply stand them up in the pots. Usually, they work better if I keep the mix simple so it isn't too busy, combining a broadleaf or two with a couple of conifers. As with wreaths, I aim for a variety of textures: some pine and juniper branches perhaps, a little boxwood, twigs of berried holly, the dangling tassels of pieris. Poked into moist soil and freeze-framed by winter's chill, they stay fresh for months. (Broadleaf evergreens benefit from Wilt-Pruf, an antitranspirant that slows evaporation and helps their foliage stay plump.) Most of the time I just arrange the branches as artfully as I can in urns, troughs, and other containers and then just walk away. But if I'm very inspired, I fiddle with embellishments for more striking effects. I may jazz them up with dried allium heads and other seedpods spray-painted red or white. Winding grapevines through the greens is less colorful, but the result is delightfully rustic.

On the terrace off my neighbor's sunporch where she often entertains or sits and reads a book, I poked large branches of rhododendron, inkberry, and pieris into her large urns. They lasted all winter. The urns were directly in her view to the bay and added cheery comfort to the winter scene. Empty urns have the opposite effect, drawing attention to what is missing.

Greens are also ideal for hanging baskets. I line my open-weave, lichen green wire ones with moss first, then put in blocks of dampened floral foam. (I did the same thing with an iron rod planter box attached to the carpentry shed.) Since I want material that droops over the perimeter, I prefer the softer, more feathery greens: cedar, white pine, and golden chamaecyparis. Strands of variegated ivy cascading over the sides or twining through the display lend texture and light. Once I get them in place, I'll intersperse stiffer branches such as holly or boxwood as well as clutches of colorful berries to fill the middle. For more of a flourish, I might add the papery silver pods of honesty (*Lunaria*), sometimes spray-painted

OPPOSITE: On the terrace of Patricia Altschul's sunporch, the massive urns are never empty. They are a focal point for the view out the window. In summer they are filled with flowers, and in winter they overflow with assorted greens. It's a great way to bring the outside in.

gold, and splice them in here and there. Honesty wanders around my woodland garden seeding itself in different spots each year, a lone plant here, another over there. It is never a nuisance and always welcome. The dried blue seed heads of sea holly (*Eryngium* sp.) are always welcome as well.

POTTED FIRS

Although tinkering with branches is quick, easy, and colorful, growing dwarf conifers in containers adds year-round interest. These slow-growing variations resemble their larger siblings (see page 37), but some only shoot up a couple of inches per year, so they can live happily in the same container for many years or for a season before you move them into the garden. I filled a miniature footed bathtub with dwarfs and it was a humorous addition to the terrace throughout the year. Larger conifers still make ideal companions for containers, if the

Empty urns have the opposite effect,

container is large enough to allow them room for growth. Even quick-growing coni-fers in their infancy can fill the bill for a season or two before being moved into a more permanent place in the garden. I've been both surprised and pleased to find a wonderful inexpensive assortment at Home Depot. Winter-blooming bulbs can be tucked in around them to add to the show.

Position a pair of containers at the head of a walk, the bottom of stairs or on each side of an entry or a driveway. Cluster a group on a terrace or a porch. Individual pots can be dotted throughout the garden to add interest to dormant beds. A large pot with a specimen conifer can be a focal point at the end of a path. I particularly like **dwarf Alberta spruce (*Picea glauca* 'Conica')** for its classic cone shape; **Colorado blue spruce (*Picea pungens* 'Bakeri')** for its luscious blue-green color; **lemon cypress (*Cupressus* 'Golden Wilma')** with its golden green foliage and lemon scent; and *Pinus cembra* **'Nana'** for its long soft needles and pyramid form. For something low and domelike—and golden to boot—you can't top *Thuga plicata* **'Cuprea',** a dwarf western red cedar.

A metal window box is filled with branches of rose hips, holly berries, Oriental spruce 'Skyland', and other evergreens including the red foliage of *Nandina* 'Wood's Dwarf'. OPPOSITE, LEFT TO RIGHT: A miniature footed bathtub is filled with dwarf conifers and holly clippings surrounding a lemon cypress; a golden Italian cypress glows behind a pot combining *Miscanthus* and Mexican feather grass and kale. A few pine branches were poked in for more winter interest.

drawing attention to what is missing.

CLOCKWISE, FROM BOTTOM LEFT: A metal standing basket is lined with moss and filled with moist soil for branches of rhododendron, holly, juniper, rose hips, and golden conifers to be poked in; a fiberglass container is planted with variegated ivy and has assorted greens, orange holly berries, and red-twig dogwood poked in behind; a copper hanging basket holds an assortment of golden conifers, holly, and greens.

OPPOSITE: Branches of blue spruce, juniper, variegated holly, and rhododendron fill a wicker hanging basket lined with moss. Stems of red holly berries and rose hips are added as a finishing touch.

WINDOW-BOX WONDERS

Speaking of conifers, the really small ones referred to by the American Conifer Society as miniatures, are great for window boxes, although any baby conifer works for a season. For Christmas cheer, they can be trimmed with tiny ornaments or strings of lights. A row of 12-inch-high globe-shaped **little-leaf boxwood (*Buxus microphylla* 'Kingswood Dwarf')** makes a stunning, formal statement, while mixing different petite forms of Hinoki false cypress gives a more casual look. A series of these make a window box look like a scaled-down forest.

Decorative evergreen groundcovers that drape over the side of containers have a softening effect. Two good choices are ***Euonymus fortunei* 'Moonshadow'** with its green leaves and golden streaks and ***Gaultheria procumbens* 'Wintergreen'** with its glossy little green leaves and bright red berries. Either one could be planted around the base of a large conifer. Add early-blooming bulbs and it's a garden in a pot.

MOVABLE BULBS

Most autumns I plant a couple of whisky barrels, a child-size wheelbarrow, and all-weather containers with early-blooming bulbs: snowdrops, eranthis, perhaps some scilla or muscari. Some I've topped with quick-growing rye grass so the bulbs bloom through the grass. I cover the top of the pots with chicken wire to keep out the squirrels and then I put them outside and forget about them until it is time for them to bloom. Since they're against the wall of the house or in the sunny vegetable garden, they usually burst into bloom sooner than the bulbs I've planted in the garden. If I want to hurry them up, I move them into the greenhouse after they have had a cool 2-month, outdoor nap. Like magic, they quickly sprout and bloom. It is a good show for children.

Once the bulbs come into bloom, I move them around the yard or into the house where they will be seen and enjoyed. After they have passed their prime, I transplant them into a permanent place in the garden. They don't mind all the movement and I don't mind the extra work. In spring, I can more easily see where they will make a difference the following winter. Often in fall the gardens are so crowded that it is hard to remember where flowers are needed.

A children's wooden wheelbarrow is planted with crocus and can be moved into the garden where color is needed. OPPOSITE: A metal window box is planted with dwarf conifers including *Chamaecyparis lawsoniana* 'Ellwoodii', lemon cypress, Juniper 'Blue Star', and a dwarf Alberta spruce. Beauty berries are poked in to add more color.

Ice and Fire

Winters are long and cold in Willow, Alaska, 70 miles north of Anchorage. "A far cry from the rough and tumbleweed Texas where I was born," says Les Brake. He loved Alaska the moment he set foot there in 1980 and moved up permanently in 1984. The mountains at his back gave him a sense of security, rather than the wide open Texas plains.

But Les soon discovered that an Alaskan summer—with galloping growth, constant sunshine, and gorgeous flowers—is extremely different from a winter. "Here temperatures vary 145 degrees between the seasons with the coldest day at −55°F and the warmest at 90°F," says Les. "Winter is so brutally cold for so long that the woodshed is bigger than our house." Outdoor gardening begins in May when the snow melts and runs through late August when frost returns.

After his first winter, Les was starved for flowers and color so he planted an extraordinary garden that over the years has only grown better. He holds an open house in August that attracts hundreds of visitors. In the winter he starts seeds indoors and prepares what he can for May planting. But starting plants and tending his wood fire wasn't enough to fight the gloom. So to make winter bearable when there was only a couple of hours of daylight, Les began making "fire in ice"—elaborate frozen shapes lit from within by candles. For the holidays he lines his 140-foot driveway with the ice shapes and decorates his porch to view the candles from inside the house. As word spread around his small town about what he was doing, visitors came to see. Consequently,

Les was inspired to make more ice art.

In 2006 he made more than 125 "fire in ice" designs. As he wrote, "I usually say ice arrangements, but that doesn't explain the candles. It's the fire in ice thing that makes this so magical. They're not ice sculptures because I'm not using chisels, chain saws, or propane torches. They're not luminaries because, well, that word just isn't right for something made in the deep North. Besides, luminaries are just candles in bags—a fire hazard. What I'm doing, though, is fire in ice."

To shape the ice, Les searches thrift shops and borrows containers from his kitchen. He lines up his molds on the porch and carries water from the kitchen to fill them up. His watering can never rests. Once the forms are partially frozen, he adds a few drops of food coloring. If he added the coloring to the water, the color would be too even and would not create interesting patterns. Initially, he only mixed in blue food coloring since ice often has a bluish cast. Later he branched out using every color imaginable, even yellow despite the fact that yellow snow has a bad connotation.

The molds vary from standard bowls, Bundt and cake pans, to plastic bags. He found a plastic moon-shaped platter and another diamond shape

(continued)

OPPOSITE: Each side of this box of ice was frozen separately with colorful ice cubes added to the water. The sides were then "glued" together with a slush of snow. A candle lights it from the middle.

that he brings out yearly. A favorite is his deep-dish, nonstick cookie sheet.

He also finds possibilities where others see trash. Les discovered that if he poured water into a plastic banana bag and hung it up, when he unmolded it, it had the shape of a flame. He explained, "I'm trying to find the inner beauty of everything, including banana bags and cat-litter pails. It's taking the ordinary and trying to turn it into the sublime. Once I got hooked on ice I could see shapes everywhere I looked." When he received an order of votive candles in a plastic carton, the carton became a mold. "It's another good factory shape for me, because I have five of the cartons and can really crank out the pieces with them," he wrote. "The top gets used, too, for a simple small rectangle. When it was really cold, I was getting 20 pieces of ice a day," he added. Some of the more interesting shapes with scalloped edges he makes with a 5-gallon bucket,

"Winter is so brutally cold for so long that

tipping it on all four "sides", inserting colored cubes at the base when the ice starts to thicken on each wall. Colored ice cubes are frequently frozen into other molds to add depth and texture.

A neighbor asked him where he got the mold for icicles—incredible but true. He simply breaks them off of his back shed and stands them upside down in mounds of snow. Snow is the glue that holds many of his shapes together.

Of course, most of his work is done outside,

ABOVE, LEFT TO RIGHT: The way to Les's house and barn glows from the lights of a sampling of his ice sculptures. The ones in front are made from jelly molds; the flame-shaped ice candles are formed in hanging plastic banana bags.
OPPOSITE, LEFT TO RIGHT: Les Brake drinks his coffee as he looks over his "fire in ice" show; a ring of upside-down icicles stands in the snow, lit by a candle within.

and sadly Les has permanent frostbite damage on several of his fingers from working outdoors when it was -30°F. He wrote in January 2006: "Average temperature for the month has been about 0°

(continued)

the woodshed is bigger than our house."

(that's nothing, eh?), so I've cranked out enough ice to have 90 or so pieces to light. I've never done anything quite like this before, and it's exhilarating to have the opportunity to put on such a show that will spotlight Alaska as the totally unique place that it is. The temperature never went above zero on Thursday, and I spent 8 hours outside "gluing" most of the shapes together that needed it with a slurry of snow and ice water. That's the fun part, and I was just loving putting it all together. Finished up that phase for the most part Friday night after midnight. Don't worry; it was a balmy 4° above."

Les's secret to unmolding the ice shapes without having them crack is to bring them indoors and let them slowly melt until they easily slide out on their own. It usually takes a half-hour. Les doesn't recommend running hot water over the molds. They melt too fast and often crack.

In the course of a winter, Les can burn more than 600 candles. He relights them every day and blows them out when he goes to bed. Backing up to a wilderness, he is always on the alert for any roaming wild animals when he ventures out, even on his deck.

Since the ice and fire show is something the town looks forward to, Les starts making his sculptures in mid-November and continues right up until Christmas, sometimes even into January. If he is lucky and the winter temperatures hold, the ice art lasts the whole winter. In 2005 he lost a bunch when a "pineapple express" blew in on January 2 with rain and warm temperatures. But nothing stops Les, although it might slow him down a bit. Melded into Les the gardener and the ice artist is Alaska's frontier spirit, which will carry him beautifully through all kinds of extreme weather.

OPPOSITE: Ice bowls molded in all different sizes and colored with food coloring are "glued" together with snow to create this contemporary ice sculpture.

ICE IS NICE

Inspired by pictures from Alaskan gardener Les Brake, last year I experimented with making some of my own ice candles and decorations. My foray into ice imagery is easy enough for anyone.

I fitted a small plastic cup—large enough to hold a pillar candle—into a larger can, then filled it with stones, although any weight would do. The stones held down the small cup and kept it from floating up when I added water. I filled the bottom third of the larger can with water and added sprigs of holly with clusters of berries. I put it all into the freezer for an hour or so until it set, as I wanted to be sure that the holly would stay at the bottom and not float up. Then I filled up the larger can almost to the top with water. Once it was frozen solid, I let it sit in the kitchen sink for a half-hour to slowly melt until I could separate the vessels. I placed my ice mold out in the frozen garden and lit the candle inside it before my company arrived. It greeted guests as they walked in.

One winter I used a birdbath as a pedestal to hold a twig tree that I decorated. One of the sillier trees I did was hung with acorns frozen in ice cubes along with balls of birdseed for a decorative effect.

A pair of these iron urns is filled with assorted evergreens, conifers, and holly berries to dress up our entrance.

OPPOSITE: A decorative urn in the fragrance garden at the Denver Botanic Garden is filled with cut evergreens and corkscrew willow (*Salix matsudana* 'Koidzumi').

IT'S ELEMENTAL

These days you can find planters made from a multitude of materials and in all price ranges. While I still prefer classic terra-cotta and pottery in the summer garden, here in the Northeast, those pots are liable to crack during winter. I got tired of dragging all the heavy pots inside every November. If I leave them out, I cover them in black plastic so they won't fill with water, freeze, and break. It isn't particularly attractive but it works in far corners of the garden that are not often visited by guests in the winter. I've switched over to those made of resin, cement, plastic, or fiberglass for winter containers. There are actually gorgeous terra-cotta and cement fakes, if chosen carefully, and they are a heck of a lot easier to move around.

Cast iron. A combination of different irons that have been melted and then cast into forms such as urns with intricate shapes and detailing; extremely durable and weather resistant; imparts a stately, vintage look; good water retention but no breathability; very heavy so best positioned where it won't need to be moved; usually does not have drainage holes

Cement or concrete. Crushed rock mixtures with a rough texture that are very durable; heavy; fairly cold resistant; may chip or break; porous; rustic, earthy look; relatively inexpensive compared to other containers

Fiberglass, resin, plastic polyethylene. Man-made materials which can be formulated to resemble stone, terra-cotta, cast iron; strong, durable, lightweight and weather resistant; vary greatly in quality, with some styles fairly screaming "fake" and others offering high-class imagery; good water retention but no breathability

Terra-cotta. Clay pottery in a muted rust color that looks good in the landscape; the natural porosity means the pot can dispel any excess water (the reason you often see "water lines" on its surface); clay also helps the potted plant's root system to breathe; heavy and hard to move; may break or chip; not resistant to freezing temperatures

Zinc. Natural material with a dark gray color that resembles lead; used for centuries in Europe for statuary and planters and now quite popular in sleek, modern shapes; fairly lightweight; won't rust or discolor; does not breathe and may need to be drilled for drainage holes

Juniperus chinensis 'Torulosa' grows in an iron urn and is decorated for the holidays with dried alliums sprayed red. OPPOSITE: A bird topiary sits on a post at an entrance to a home in Cooperstown, New York.

IN THE POT

Although I've mentioned several dwarf conifers well-suited to containers, there are many more conifers and evergreens to choose from. Junipers, for example, are very accommodating. Here are some other possibilities:

Common boxwood (*Buxus sempervirens*). Boxwood has long been a favorite container plant because it is slow growing, doesn't mind being confined, and can be clipped into interesting shapes. I love the plain green but am intrigued with ones with variegated foliage: 'Marginata' has dark green leaves rimmed in yellow; 'Elegantissima' bears very narrow, white-margined leaves; 'Latifolia Maculata' starts off yellow, then turns dark green with yellow markings. All of these won't top 10 feet and are easily pruned.

***Cupressus macrocarpa* 'Goldcrest'.** This Monterey cypress is a favorite for topiaries that look splendid in containers. The naturally conical form is an excellent base for coaxing into 5-foot tall spirals and the leaves are a wonderful golden color. *C. sempervirens* (Italian cypress) is also frequently used for topiary art.

***Euonymus japonicus* 'Silver Princess'.** I have several varieties of euonymus growing in the garden as groundcovers and shrubs, but this variegated cultivar, with its graceful globe shape, is perfect in a pot. The dark green leaves are outlined with a white line that makes it positively sparkle.

***Ilex crenata* 'Sky Pencil'.** This Japanese holly is as skinny as a fashion model and just as chic with lustrous dark green leaves and dark purple berries. It can reach 10 feet tall, but is perfectly happy a few feet shorter, doing its thing in an elegant square container.

English yew (*Taxus baccata*). Although yews are usually sold as foundation plantings, some of the smaller cultivars are fine in containers. The fact that they adapt easily to extensive shearing means you can have a neat flat-topped shrub or a gently rounded one.

Pots for All Seasons

Dennis Schrader, a wholesale nursery grower in Long Island, placed a few potted plants to hide the glaring white steps to his side door. He arranged them so their colors repeated, at different levels, as they "bounced" down the stairs. He quickly discovered that walking by the pots "put a smile on my face every time I went to work and returned home." Consequently, he always keeps pots on the steps, even in winter.

Dennis lives in Zone 7 but specializes in tropical plants. Since his greenhouse and office are near his house, he often returns home several times a day. As he explained, "When you walk by plants several times a day, you get to know them intimately." Dennis credits the plants on his stoop for making him a better plantsman.

Winter, understandably, is the toughest season. Fewer plants can stand having their roots frozen. The mixture of plants climbing the steps includes shrubs, perennials, and grasses that are not commonly grown in pots but can stand up to winter. As Dennis said, "We are all tempted to buy shrubs when they are in flower, but they are often so small that they make a puddle rather than a splash in the garden." On the steps, they are front and center, more easily seen, and appreciated in their youth. Azalea, cryptomeria, holly, nandina, skimmia, dwarf rhododendron, and juniper are a few of the shrubs Dennis plumps up in pots before planting into the garden. His dwarf Alberta spruces have grown in black plastic buckets for 10 years, only once trading up in pot size.

Foliage beauties such as *Sedum* 'Angelina', the more common hens and chicks, and *Carex flagellifera* 'Toffee Twist' look good for four seasons. Although 'Toffee Twist', with its brunet twirling locks, makes every day look like a bad-hair day, it is so beloved by gardeners.

Dennis even keeps pots of strawflowers, dried on dead stems. And why not? It is easier than moving them into a vase and they still look good. He also uses cut branches of winterberry, magnolia, and holly to poke in around plants and places noble fir, incense cedar, and spruce on the ground between the pots.

Dennis cautions that even in winter, if the sun is shining on the pots, they need moderate watering. He also cautions that when water freezes in a pot, it expands and could break the pot unless it is frost-proof. To protect his pots, he puts a piece of old garden hose across the bottom inside each one before planting it. The empty hose squashes together when the water freezes, alleviating pressure on the pot's sides.

As Dennis says, "The colors, scents, and textures of plants arranged artfully make a beautiful transition from one season to another." It is certainly worth the trouble of seeking out plants for all seasons.

OPPOSITE: At Dennis Schrader and Bill Smith's home, pots of assorted plants decorate the steps year-round. In winter, dwarf conifers, evergreens, and grasses live in the pots accented by cut branches of holly and berries. Dried flowers grown in the pots over the summer stay through the winter. Even though the plants are dead, the flowers look perfect.

Christmas from the Garden

A house festooned with nature's bounty—evergreens, dried flowers, pinecones, seedpods, and berries—takes the chill off the season, warming everyone who steps inside. And the spicy fragrance of pines perfumes the house. Nature's gifts, with their simple dignity, are

OPPOSITE: Ron Solt's wreaths are unique for their wide variety of textures and colors. Included here are assorted green and variegated hollies including yellow holly berries, 'Skyland' spruce, Korean fir, *Pierus japonica* 'Dorothy Wycoff', and red tiger-eye pine.

153

beautiful alone or costumed with red ribbons and ornaments.

Consequently, holiday decorations cut from the garden are a tradition at our house. It all started when my four kids were young. In addition to unpacking the boxes of ornaments and ribbons that were stored in the attic, I would grab a basket and wander through the woods and garden, cutting boughs and berries and collecting pods and pinecones to bring inside to deck the house. As my children grew, the wonder, excitement, and anticipation reflected in their faces when we decorated used to spur me on to overdress the house. Now that they are grown, I simply can't help myself.

I start dressing the house in early December, extending the enjoyment and eliminating drudgery by decorating a little at a time. On pleasant days, I trim boxwood hedges and prune pine trees and broadleaf evergreens. The clippings are combined into wreaths, swags, centerpieces, and mantel displays. The possibilities for natural decorations from the garden are endless. By pairing different textures and colors—the large dark green rosettes of rhododendron leaves, tiny blushing azalea foliage, spiny sprigs of shiny holly, soft piles of fir, drapes of golden cedar, and bristly blue spruce—rich effects can be achieved. Add to this the seasonal berries of holly, barberry, rose hips, juniper, bittersweet, and winterberries, as well as dried seedpods and flowers. There are so many plants to work with. Use whatever you can find in your garden or perhaps from a friendly neighbor's yard in the dead of night (I won't tell). While you're at it, assess if there is room for another evergreen or two in your own garden to enhance your pickings in years to come.

Cut greens that hold their needles or foliage the longest out of water include juniper, leucothoe, euonymus, spruce, boxwood, bergenia, lavender, arborvitae, pine, laurel, rhododendron, holly, ivy, and evergreen magnolia. If you're grouping a mixture in water for a dining table, entrance, or mantel, keep in mind that all last for 10 days to 2 weeks. Some boxwood, balsam, and assorted pines have the extra kick of scenting the air. And don't forget bare branches—ones with twisted shapes are interesting in arrangements or on their own with ornaments dangling from them.

I also rely on dried seed heads as embellishments:

OPPOSITE: A pair of potted Christmas trees sits on a mat of greens. Their diminutive size emphasizes the massive and majestic conifers beyond.

LIVE CHRISTMAS TREES

Conifers are available at discounted prices in November and December, a good time to buy them. The assortment of live trees in pots and burlap comes in a wider array of colors than cut Christmas trees. They can be placed indoors for a few weeks or outdoors in containers for the holidays. When the season has passed, they can be planted into a permanent place in the garden. Some such as Alberta spruce can live for many years in containers.

When grown indoors for a few weeks, conifers need to be watered regularly, keeping the soil evenly moist. They, too, can be decorated in the same way as cut trees. Once the season has past, the trees need to be moved outdoors where they will still need to be watered if the weather is dry. Once the ground has thawed, they can planted into the ground.

If the trees are used for outdoor decoration, they can be planted where color is needed most, flanking the walk to the front door, lining the driveway or the front steps, or even enhancing a garden.

I often place a pair decorated with lights for the holidays on each side of the entrance and later plant them where they are needed for privacy along our property line the following spring. Some slow growers, such as Alberta spruce and boxwood, can live for many happy years in containers. In Cooperstown, New York, where the whole town takes pride in its outdoor holiday show (see page 188), the boxwood topiary is always a scene stealer.

Some, such as the black balls of black-eyed Susans, honey brown spiky sweet-gum balls, brown velvety stars of tree peonies, and red pearls of multiflora rose hips, I pick straight from the winter garden. Others—allium, globe amaranth, sea holly, assorted salvia, and hydrangea—I gather over the summer and hang in the garden house to dry. Celosias, especially the plush, red velvety ones, are very festive. If you don't grow your own, you can easily purchase them at craft stores, nurseries, or florists.

DECK THE HALLS

Each year I try new things as well as repeat favorites from years before. Here are some of the ways I've decorated our house in past years. I don't do everything every year. How could I? I do as much as I enjoy doing and as time allows. But whatever I do makes a big difference in how cheerful our house is in December.

The twisted bare branches of a willow tree are decorative in their own right but more so when dressed with ornaments for the holidays.
OPPOSITE: After clamping a 6-inch-wide piece of chicken wire long enough to reach the floor to the mantel, I tied on fan-shaped branches of noble fir, starting from the bottom and overlapping to create a draping effect, as if a shawl was flung off to the side. A garland of silver stars adds glitter.

One-of-a-Kind Wreaths and Swags

There's no rhyme or reason to the way I deck the halls. Each year is different. I take my inspiration from what I've gathered and often begin with the embellishments. I might take the seed heads of allium and spray-paint them red or white and sprinkle them with glitter. Or I wire the bottoms of pinecones so they'll be at the ready for affixing to wreaths and garlands. Left as is, dusted with gold or tipped with silver, these are always cheery accents. Or I might spend a pleasant half-hour simply wiring together bunches of berries, pods, dried flowers, and bits of boxwood. A box of choice ornaments nearby sparks an idea for different color themes . . . a red-feathered bird suggests a classic Christmas theme perhaps, or maybe a blue star will inspire something celestial. Just looking at what I've gathered prompts lots of ideas.

Once I've fiddled and tweaked, I usually begin by making some wreaths. Nothing signals Christmas like seeing greenery on doors and windows and as centerpieces. Although I decorate mostly round wreaths in different sizes for different purposes, I also include a square wreath or two. Before I was able to find square wire forms at a

floral supply store, I used old wooden picture frames as bases. Clusters of greens or moss can be glued or stapled onto the wood rather than wired into place. A simple wreath, for indoors or out, is made covering the frame with sheets of dried moss, gluing on some sprigs of rose hips (a favorite food of birds), and topping it off with a red bird decoration or two. It's a wreath with a theme—feed the birds in winter.

The round metal frames come in a large assortment of sizes. The traditional way to decorate them is with evergreens (see page 165). Last year instead of using a base of conifers, I used dried bunches of baby's breath that had been sprayed with glitter. I overlapped them as I moved around the frame until it was completely covered. Surprisingly the dried stems bent easily without breaking, following the curves of the frame. It hung over the dining room fireplace and sparkled in the evenings reflecting the candlelight. It worked so well that I asked a friend to cut a star template out of wood. I wired more baby's breath around it in the same manner and hung it outside on the front balcony. It lasted for months despite the bad weather. Because the baby's breath was bright white, it glowed in the evening. No lights were needed.

Ready-made grapevine wreaths come in assorted sizes and are also handy. I have a few I reuse from season to season. In winter I can wire on seed pods, acorns, and dried flowers and hang it in the garden until spring. I made one for Thanksgiving one year and left it up until spring because it looked good and matched the dried seed heads and grasses still standing in the garden.

In Cooperstown, New York, they often hang wreaths outdoors made entirely of dried flowers, and they look wonderful for the season. My favorite borrowed idea is that of a dried flower wreath set on top of a container on an entrance pillar. Looking a little like the letter O, it really stands out. It could be attached to metal poles stuck deep in the pot, one on each side. Of course, it has to be decorated on both sides so you can enjoy the flowers both coming and going. The same idea can be put into practice with any wreath. It is so much more noticeable when it stands on a pillar.

I keep a supply of floral foam wreath forms in assorted sizes for most of my wreath making. Greens last longer in the moist foam. The foam forms are also useful

A wooden template of a star is covered with overlapping bunches of dried baby's breath. Thin wire holds it in place and is almost invisible. Sprayed-on gold glitter adds sparkle.

OPPOSITE: A juniper wreath decorated with dried cockscomb is balanced on top of a pillar in Cooperstown, New York.

throughout the year to display flowers on the garden gate or on a table encircling a cache of votives or a single candle pillar. However, on a door that is regularly opened and might be accidentally slammed closed by a child or the wind, they might break. In those situations, I use wire forms or grapevine wreaths.

To use a handy foam device, which is mounted on a lightweight round plastic tray, first float the form in water with a packet of floral preservative mixed in. Once the foam is saturated, you're good to go. Cut evergreen stems on a sharp angle so they can be inserted into the foam without breaking. Poke through to the middle of the foam but not out the other side. Cover the ring completely with fir and then spruce it up with other garden clippings.

Of course, the easier way to make a wreath is to start with one from the Christmas tree lot. It's an inexpensive canvas on which to embroider greens and berries from the garden. A roll of floral green wire is all that's needed to secure items; the rest is up to

Nothing signals Christmas like seeing

you. I always plump out the existing wreath with more greenery, weaving in different textures to make it fuller, and add a few rose hips and berries for splashes of subtle color. Fresh flowers are another terrific enhancement. Small roses, carnations, lilies, and amaryllis can be inserted into small water-filled vials and wired onto the wreath. (If you're using a foam form, simply push the stems into it). There's nothing like a lush green wreath studded with candy-striped amaryllis to elicit oohs and aahs. And oddly enough, cut amaryllis flowers placed in water last a whole lot longer than those on live plants.

Bows are optional. I feel that they can sometimes distract from the natural appeal of a straight-from-the-garden wreath. Tassels, braid, or velvet cord often do the job better. However,

(continued on page 166)

THROUGH A GLASS BRIGHTLY

Why settle for placing Christmas flowers into vases filled with water when you can go one better? A clear cylinder filled with fresh cranberries is a knockout vessel for bold red amaryllis. Ditto an inexpensive garland of pearls sold to decorate a Christmas tree can be bunched in the bottom of a glass vase to cradle pristine paperwhites. Other fillers include clear or colored marbles, gold or silver beads, lemons, and limes. Besides adding pizzazz to the vases, these extras also help hold the stems in place.

greenery on doors, windows, and tables.

A Wreath of Many Colors

Until I met Ron Solt, I thought I was pretty good at constructing holiday wreaths. Ron, though, is a true expert. Owner of a nursery and flower shop in Barto, Pennsylvania, he turns to his own arboretum of conifers and evergreens, especially hollies, to create circles of unusual beauty. "Anything you can cut fresh is better than what you can buy," he states. "The greens sold at most home centers are cut in late September, then shipped and held for months before they come on the market. No wonder they dry out so soon." So take a tip from Ron and look to your own garden for the ingredients to make indoor arrangements.

Whether Ron is making a wreath, swag, or centerpiece, he knows the importance of mixing textures and assorted shades of green. He may start with classic pine boughs, then spike the greens with gold or blue foliage and variegated ivy leaves, fill them in with some cedar clippings, and add highlights of red or yellow berries. The idea is to mix, not match, and to have fun with all kinds of clippings.

In the classes he teaches to garden clubs, Ron demonstrates different approaches. The classic technique is to make nosegays of an assortment of 6- to 8-inch greens in your hand, wrap a wire around their base, fan them out, then wire the bunch to the wreath frame. Ron keeps making bunches and adding them to the frame, always moving in the same direction until the frame is completely covered. The top of each bunch covers the base of the one it overlapped. Usually six or eight bunches are needed, depending on the size of the wreath and the fullness of the bunches. Once the wire frame is completely covered, berries, rose hips, ornaments, dried flowers, or anything else that might perk it up can be wired together in small bunches, then inserted. Ron's wreaths always stand out because of the unique mixture he uses of gold and blue conifers with broadleaf evergreens.

However, to retain maximum freshness, Ron favors this old-fashioned method.

1. Begin by filling a metal wreath frame with soggy sphagnum moss that's been soaked overnight in a bucket of water. Wire the moss in place, then wrap all around the frame with 3-inch-wide green plastic wrap (it looks like plastic ribbon and is available from floral supply companies). Continue wrapping a second time and affix into place with a twist of wire. (The first wrap will hold the wet moss in place and the second should cover the seams, preventing leaks and evaporation.)

2. Before inserting greens into the form, remove the needles from the bottom 2 inches of the branches. Poke holes into the wreath with a pencil or thin dowel to make placement easier. Ron uses a metal pic machine that attaches a metal point to the base of each stem. It makes it easier to insert through the plastic and making holes ahead of time is not necessary.

3. Start by inserting fir branches about 6 inches long with at least a half-dozen ltips. Always working in the same direction, overlap the branches slightly until the entire base is covered. Once you have a plush fir base, the fun begins.

4. Now put in your other, more unconventional greens. Weeping Nootka cypress, white pine, or cedar all lend texture, while golden greens add sunshine. Ron recommends *Juniperus* 'Saybrook Gold', golden Serbian spruce, and *Pinus strobus* 'Hillside Gold'.

5. For more dimension, add a few sprigs of holly, laurel, or boxwood.

6. Berries give needed flashes of color, but sometimes they get lost in the overall arrangement, so Ron usually removes their foliage. Just insert as above on top of other leaves.

7. As you work, the size of the wreath will expand—that 16-inch wire form will become a 24- to 26-inch wreath—so plan accordingly when you begin and make sure the greens are evenly spaced.

If the wreath is not going to be hung right away, Ron suggests keeping it fresh by placing it within dampened newspapers and keeping it in a cool spot like a garage. The same method works for fresh greens simply wired on a frame.

Yes, this takes more effort than simply buying a wreath, but it is also more fun. The finished product stays fresh for weeks and weeks, much longer than a store-bought one. And you'll have something that's one-of-a-kind.

Ron's completed wreath is made of magnolia leaves, Korean fir, Fraser fir, golden arborvitae, and variegated tiger-eye pine. The orange berries are *Ilex* 'Aurantiaca', a deciduous holly.
OPPOSITE: Ron Solt making a moss-filled wreath base in his greenhouse.

There are so many variations on how to make a Christmas wreath. Any of these would also be wonderful on a table as a centerpiece with a candle in the center.

ABOVE, CLOCKWISE FROM TOP LEFT: Fraser fir, magnolia leaves, pinecones, and berries decorate this wreath; dried flowers including yarrow and hydrangea, holly berries, rose hips, bird nests, pinecones, and wheat are wired onto a straw base; moss covers a wooden picture frame decorated with rose hips and a cardinal.

OPPOSITE, CLOCKWISE FROM TOP LEFT: A wreath of golden conifers and holly hangs around a lantern; a wreath with everything picked from the garden in February includes variegated euonymus, cyclamen, rose hips, and lavender; a wreath of mixed green and gold conifers dusted with snow on a garden gate; a wreath of assorted greens and holly with viburnum berries.

A swag made by designer Gina Norgard includes branches of tiger-eye pine, holly, blue spruce, and pinecones.

OPPOSITE: Green garlands complete the decoration at the entrance to this house by visually tying the pair of topiaries to the wreath on the front door.

if a bow is necessary, use really good ribbon. Although taffeta, satin, and grosgrain are gorgeous, wired varieties are easiest to work with. Just don't skimp on the quantity; you want the bow to be in scale with the wreath and to look totally luxurious.

The same principle of combining assorted evergreens works for swags and garlands as well. Rather than taking the time to wire together barrels of prunings, I cut corners by buying garlands of white pine or cedar. Most nurseries and tree markets sell these in 10- and 25-yard lengths and they're prime for preening. I usually wire on bunches of other greens every 12 inches or so and add berries, flowers, or small clusters of pinecones.

Another inexpensive accent is crystal chandelier drops. I picked up a few dozen of these at a flea market, knowing I could use them for something, and voila! These baubles have holes at the top and sometimes wire fasteners so they're easy to affix to branches. They make perfect "icicles" for swags and garlands and give a subtle shimmer reminiscent of ice.

Garlands wrapped around lampposts and mailboxes and strung across balconies may be old-fashioned but they do perk up the winter scene.

Crystal chandelier drops make perfect "icicles" for swags and give a subtle shimmer reminiscent of ice.

The golden light on this
perfectly shaped conifer
warms the winter scene.

169

An individual favor of holiday greens made in a mint julep cup is placed at each table setting.

OPPOSITE, CLOCKWISE FROM TOP LEFT: A small tree is decorated with dried flowers; a tree of dried hydrangea, red alliums, salvia, and gomphrena; a boxwood tree, made by poking stems of boxwood into a triangle of floral foam, is decorated with rose hips and acorn ornaments; a rose tree made on a base of floral foam has a ribbon of variegated ivy and rests in a pot covered with ivy leaves.

O Christmas Tree, O Christmas Tree

To my mind, you can never have enough Christmas trees—little ones here and there to decorate every nook and cranny. I cut blocks of floral foam into triangles, with the point up, anywhere from 4 inches to 1 foot high. After soaking the foam, I poke in boxwood stems, using larger twigs at the bottom and ending with shorter pieces. As I stick in the stems, I round out the form. At the very tip, I point one stem straight up to emphasize the top of the tree. The trees are considerably bigger than the floral foam form when I finish. A series of small ones, only about 6 inches high, make adorable favors on a holiday table. I nestle them in inexpensive silver julep cups at each place setting.

Red rosebuds or small red carnations (easily found at the supermarket) also make fabulous mini trees. Again, just dampen the floral-foam triangle and stick the stems of the flowers directly into it. For a contrasting natural garland, I twirl a length of 'Goldheart' or variegated ivy from the garden around it.

My real showstopper tree is a 3-footer, made entirely of dried hydrangea heads. I snip the flowers in early fall when they feel slightly leathery and still display blue-green color and let them dry naturally, hanging upside down in bunches in the garden house. Then I push the flower heads between the branches of a twig tree form. It doesn't take much time—a half-hour at most. The hydrangea blooms completely cover the form, and the various shades of blue and green in the dried flowers are the perfect palette for adding ornaments or more dried flowers to gussy it up. I've poked in rose hips, dried rosebuds, and even dried allium heads spray-painted red. A mix of assorted dried flowers can make the tree more interesting.

You can also decorate a real Christmas tree with hydrangeas—and you won't need as many! Tuck the flower heads in between the branches, add other ornaments such as silver-dusted allium (I like *Allium shuberti*, which resembles an airy puff of fireworks), silvery pods of honesty, and dried rosebuds. A berried garland is the perfect finishing touch.

Last but not least is what I call my "bare-bones" trees, made from interesting branches that have snapped off during a winter storm. I brace each branch in a small bucket or crock filled with dampened floral foam, or if a branch is heavy, I set it in plaster of Paris; that way it can be used from year to year. I cover the base with moss and hang tiny ornaments on the branches.

Holiday Haberdashery

Any pieces of greenery left over from my clipping madness can be put to use in arrangements. An arrangement for a centerpiece, a coffee table, or a mantel can be easily made by poking decorative greens into floral foam in a colorful bowl or a plastic-lined basket. A bunch of fresh flowers or two—think red tulips or white amaryllis—is an elegant addition for Christmas. But the basic idea can be repeated all winter long for an inexpensive yet beautiful seasonal display. A bunch of flowers from the supermarket goes a long way when mixed in with garden greens. The greens last 2 or 3 weeks; the flowers only 4 or 5 days but they can be replaced with different flowers as needed.

Even snippets of greens can be parlayed into fancy finery for candlesticks. Just twist heavy-gauge wire into a circle a little larger than the candles you intend to use, then attach teeny branches of boxwood or juniper to the circle with finer-gauge floral wire. Slide these "collars" over your candles and in minutes, you've turned ordinary candlesticks into something festive and fabulous. The same mini wreaths can be used as napkin rings. Or, instead of wire rings, twist grapevine into circlets and stud with greens or berries or a single pinecone. Pinecones also do double duty as place-card holders. Just write guests' names in colored ink on small pieces of buff-colored paper or heavy vellum and insert into the pinecone.

Moss is another gift from the garden, but it's often overlooked. I simply hot-glue

pieces of moss to foam balls. They can be piled high outdoors in a birdbath or suspended, as they do in Cooperstown, from a lamppost or tree by gluing ribbon loops to their tops. They can be embroidered with dried flowers, acorns, or any other personal touches to make them original. A crisscross of thin lengths of gold cord over the balls gives a shine.

To create a centerpiece of a winter scene, I mounded rounded pieces of floral foam on a plastic tray. The foam was shaped to resemble a hilly landscape. It was then covered with sheets of moss. Small tips of conifers were stuck through the moss into the foam to resemble trees and shrubs. Small pots of mini conifers work well, too. Mini deer, fake snow, and tiny garden furniture finish it off.

If you are tired of the traditional round wreath on the front door, line an upside-down wire cone with moss instead, fill it with moist floral foam, and add greenery (see page 87). It is easier to make the arrangement in the cone while it is hanging in place. If it is hung indoors, fresh flowers can be included.

Naturally dried flowers and seed heads picked from the garden late in the season—lotus, lace-cap hydrangea, rose hips, and pinecones—can be made into beautiful long-lasting arrangements or wreaths. They can be mixed with greens for umph or left to display all the wonderful shades of tan, brown, and golden honey in Mother Nature's garden.

A winter garden is built from a mound of soil on top of a plastic tray. Miniature conifers, including *Chamaecyparis* 'Ellwoodii', are planted in the soil that is covered with moss. Golden deer, pinecones, and fake snow complete the scene.

OPPOSITE, LEFT TO RIGHT: At Old Westbury Gardens, a pot of paperwhites is covered with moss and sits on a plate of magnolia leaves; a wreath of boxwood and berries frames a votive candle.

Wrapping It Up

There's almost no end to the ways you can borrow from the garden to embellish presents. Instead of ribbon, I've tied up packages with evergreen roping or a few lengths of twisted grapevine, graced with holly. Then there's my all-time favorite ribbon—ivy vines. The strands are flexible enough to wrap and tie and the variegated forms are especially attractive. I like 'Gold Heart' (small yellow-blotched leaves with wide green border), 'Fantasia' (white and green speckled leaves), and 'Midas Touch' (golden leaves with splashes of green and a bright green rim). I've also used the same ivies for small wreaths that I tie to packages with raffia. Sometimes I simply twist the ivy around a small grapevine form, other times I use circles of floral foam. Either way, they're very pretty and always appreciated topping a special gift.

Other favorite flourishes include red dogwood twigs bent into star shapes or miniature wreaths and grapevine cones chockablock with greens and berries. The idea is to give two presents in one and have fun doing it. The package toppings can decorate the recipient's tree as well as the present. Of course, a single pinecone, dried flower, or seedpod conveys the same outdoorsy message.

Christmas Cuttings

Here are my favorite greens from the garden.

Bloomed incense cedar: Pretty green cedar with tips covered in small yellow beads; especially nice in swags and garlands

Blue-berried juniper: Attractive bluish berries are a bonus; long-lasting; adds a nice dimension to wreaths and swags

Boxwood: Small leaves on thin stems; lasts only a few weeks indoors, a month outdoors; the delicate foliage makes it ideal for small wreaths, napkin rings, or package adornments, as well as for adding contrast to larger arrangements

Cedar: Very soft, rather floppy evergreen; long-lasting with a nice sharp scent; good for lending texture and aroma to a garland

Douglas fir: Soft and flexible but short-lived; best in arrangements from which it can be easily removed and replaced

Fraser fir: Holds its form and shape for a long time; the most popular fir for wreaths

Holly: Spiny leaves mean "handle with care"; even the smallest sprigs, with or without berries, enhance anything from a garland to a wreath

Ivy: Flexible vine with leaves of varying sizes and colors; easy to work with

Magnolia: Leathery leaves are green on one side, brown on the other; long-lasting; excellent choice for subtle color in a wreath

Leucothoe fontanesiana: Branches of lance-shaped evergreen leaves in dark green, bright red, or variegated; delivers interesting texture and color to arrangements

Pieris: Long tassels of tiny blossoms surrounded by narrow leaves; lovely tucked into arrangements or wreaths

Scotch pine: Short-needled pine with Christmas aroma; adds great texture to wreaths and garlands

White pine: Long-needled pine with blue-green tinted tips; easy to work with and great as a base for garlands and wreaths; also called "Princess Pine"

TRICKS OF THE TRADE

- Dip strands of ivy in liquid floor wax to prolong their life.
- Spray broadleaf evergreens with an anti-transpirant spray such as Wilt-Pruf to slow down evaporation of moisture from their leaves.
- Substitute a lemon, an apple, or a potato for a foam ball to make a mistletoe kissing ball last.
- Condition freshly cut branches of holly by submerging them overnight in water. If arranged dry, mist them daily to keep them looking fresh.

An assortment of greens gathered from the garden sits on the workroom table. The twig tree is the base for the dried hydrangea tree (see page 171). The flower heads are simply poked into place. The mint julep cups hold triangles of floral foam that will be turned into mini trees.

At the entrance to our house the honeysuckle vines hang like curtains, so we pulled them back with red ribbon to set the stage for the holidays. The kissing ball is covered in an assortment of greens and berries and points the way to the swag on the door. Teddy, our faithful terrier, waits to greet the first guests.

179

INTERESTING TWISTS ON OUTDOOR TRADITIONS

The garden's trellises, bamboo tepees, wheelbarrows, pots, and birdbaths make original and charming outdoor holiday decorations. Simply winding tiny white lights around inexpensive bamboo tepees or metal trellises turns them into Christmas trees. And if a large pot or a birdbath is used as a pedestal with a bamboo teepee or rusted iron trellis on top, the added height makes it more noticeable.

Frost-proof birdbaths especially have multiple uses. A small cut Christmas tree decorated with lights and set into the bowl of a large birdbath lifts the tree up for all to see. The birdbath can be planted up like a pot with a garden of mini conifers or early-blooming bulbs. If the bowl isn't very deep, a collection of plants in plastic pots can be arranged inside it, with the pots covered by sheets of moss. Soil can be mounded up in the center and bulbs planted into it, or the bulbs can be in pots arranged around the conifers. There are so many variations to this idea. It is easy to take an original twist.

If the birdbath is set on the front lawn or by the door, a seasonal arrangement of greens can greet your guests. Floral frogs or foam can be taped or attached with floral clay to the bottom of the bath, so that cut branches and greens can be poked into it. Easier still is to set a basket of greens on top of the birdbath. Of course, it isn't only an idea for Christmas; it works year-round with annual flowers as well.

Dried seedpods and dried flowers can also be used to decorate outdoors. The dried heads of allium sprayed white and sprinkled with glitter resemble snowflakes. I hung some white ones in an ornamental cherry tree, and they looked beautiful for months hanging on the bare branches. I was surprised by how easily they came through several snowstorms. Sprayed red, they look like ornaments and can dress up an outdoor evergreen if wired in place. Last fall I cut down a dead conifer in the garden. It sat on the compost pile until Christmas when I noticed most of the needles had fallen off. It still had a great shape so I spray-painted it red, put it in an antique sled, and decorated it with white, glittery dried allium. It looked great, and the conifer had a life after death.

Placing a pyramid of glass ornaments in a birdbath is an idea borrowed from Elvin McDonald (see page 3). The ornaments glitter in the sunlight as if they were lit. OPPOSITE: Planting a bird-bath with early-blooming snowdrops helps the wee flowers garner some notice.

In northern climates, marginally hardy plants can be covered with greens after the first hard frost. Branches from discarded Christmas trees can be recycled this way. The layer of branches helps to protect the plants from freezing and thawing weather. A few years ago I noticed that a block in Manhattan had placed greens around the base of their street trees. The designer created a mosaic of pines including assorted greens, blue, and gold. Berries and broadleaf evergreens were woven in, and it was so beautiful that I found myself walking that block whenever possible to get another glance.

The heads of dried allium make wonderful winter decorations. They can be spray-painted any color. CLOCKWISE, FROM BOTTOM LEFT: Hanging from a tree, white alliums look like snowflakes; large white allium heads are nestled among the grasses by the pond; red alliums liven up a garland of greens over the bay window.
OPPOSITE: A dead conifer was spray-painted red after it lost its needles and was set into an antique sled where it had a second life as a Christmas tree decorated with large white alliums.

Old Westbury Gardens

In the first week of December, the greenhouse at Old Westbury Gardens in Old Westbury, New York, could easily be mistaken for Santa's workshop, although it is gardeners, not elves, frantically assembling wreaths, trees, swags, and mantel pieces to decorate the estate's house for Christmas.

My first glance through the glass revealed strange goings-on. Folding chairs were perched atop worktables, long boards balanced across their seats. Gardeners with staple guns were securing evergreens to the boards. Others were dipping pinecones, seedpods, and ornaments into an electric frying pan of hot-melt glue, then pressing them onto evergreen wreaths.

Kim Johnson, the walled-garden supervisor, explained the scene to me, as she dipped sprigs of gold-tipped incense cedar into her pan of hot-melt glue before attaching them to a board covered in blue noble fir tips. The house is a museum, so to prevent accidents, decorations are assembled in the greenhouse.

A reusable plywood template, ½ inch thick to prevent warping, has been made for each of the house's fireplace mantels. In the greenhouse, these boards are placed across chair seats or boxes on top of tables to put them at eye level, as if on the fireplaces. Greens are stapled on, ornaments glued in place, and eye hooks screwed in to hold garlands and stockings. Then these boards are trucked up to the mansion and put in place—the trickiest part, especially in bad weather.

As Kim talked, she glued on bunches of rose hips, dried red roses, and dried pomegranates.

The mantel decoration would eventually match the four wreaths she had finished earlier. The last step was lightly applying gold glitter spray (rather than a "knock-your-eyes-out, Las-Vegas style" gold) to pick up some light in the dark house. Once the board was placed on the mantel in the red ballroom, marionettes would be suspended from each side in keeping with this year's antique toy theme.

Kim cautioned anyone copying her techniques not to work while looking down upon a mantel template. Otherwise, once the board is placed on the mantel, most of what you have attached will be too high to see.

For gluing, Kim bought an electric frying pan that can maintain a low, even heat for melting hot-melt glue. The glue allows the gardeners to work faster, dipping an end of an object into the melted glue, then sticking it in place. Unlike using an old-fashioned glue gun, this is a one-handed process, and if its temperature is just above melting, the hot-melt glue quickly grabs and holds the object. And unlike a glue gun, if the hot-melt glue accidentally touches your skin, it doesn't burn.

There are many other wonderful ideas that the gardeners share each year with everyone who visits the show house in December. Scott Lucas, the greenhouse supervisor, wired overlapping

OPPOSITE: Ivy topiaries are decorated with carnations and ribbons. On the mantel, magnolia leaves, evergreens, carnations, and ribbons set the scene for a romantic Christmas.

bunches of multiflora rose hips, clipped from the wild edges of the woods, to wreath frames. He shellacked the hips to add shine and to prevent any trapped insect from hatching.

The gardens' volunteer groups join in the fun, too. They cut flowers over summer and fall, hang them to dry in an old shed, and then spray them with floral spray paint to decorate one of the indoor Christmas trees. A few years ago they had

a blue and white color scheme and spray-painted dried ornamental grass plumes blue, alliums silver, and mop-head hydrangeas an even brighter blue than what they are in the garden. It was a wonderful and creative twist on the season's decorations.

One of my favorite ideas from years past at Old Westbury Gardens is the small Christmas tree decorated with a variety of bird nests, artificial

The greenhouse at Old Westbury Gardens

birds, and dried flowers. The nests were assorted small baskets from a floral supply outlet. Some had artificial flowers attached as if the bird had woven them in. A Christmas tree decorated entirely with dried flowers and seed heads is a wonderful way to introduce birds and flowers to small children. I copied their idea for a table-top tree in our sunroom.

ABOVE, LEFT TO RIGHT: Inside an unused fireplace, an arrangement of juniper and other greens is laid on the logs, with lotus pods as the finishing touch; a foam ball covered in statice and rose hips is one of many hanging along a mantel decorated with variegated holly.
OPPOSITE, LEFT TO RIGHT: On a mantel mixed conifers and grasses are arranged in a floral foam base; a Fraser fir wreath is decorated with gilded pinecones and ribbon.

could be mistaken for Santa's workshop.

Main Street USA

Cooperstown, New York, situated around Lake Otsego, is famous for many reasons, including its "Main Street" way of life. Personally, I love the pride that the town takes in keeping its historical village and surrounding farmlands from being bought up and changed by developers. There is a lot of history in the Federal and Victorian architecture. It is a model town that "adheres to the highest standards of planning and zoning and historical preservation" as stated by its Chamber of Commerce Web site. It has all of the comforts of the modern age and the quaintness of a village.

Cooperstown first became noticed because most of James Fenimore Cooper's novels were written and set in the late 18th century in and around Cooperstown. Cooperstown was founded by his father, William Cooper, and there is a Fenimore House Museum.

Today it is probably best known by sports fans everywhere as the home of the Baseball Hall of Fame. There are so many different museums in town that it has even been dubbed "the village of museums."

In December, the combined decorating efforts of the Clark Foundation, the Scriven Foundation, Lake and Valley Garden Club, and shops, businesses, and homeowners create a magical scene. The Clark Foundation alone employs a team of 11 horticulturists to keep its historic buildings as well as the town hall decorated with seasonal plantings and holiday fare. One of the most popular events to start off the holiday is hosted by the Farmers' Museum, one of the country's oldest outdoor living history museums. It showcases rural life in 1845 in its lively village of historic trade and craft shops. Take the holiday lantern tour through the candlelit village in December to view the decorations and learn about the crafts and trades of Christmas past. It is a sight to behold!

OPPOSITE: A garland twists up a lamppost in Cooperstown. Two decorative tassels of greens hang on each side of the street sign.

Final Thoughts

What I hope you will take away from this book is a new way of looking at the winter garden and a desire to inspect yours more closely to see what is hidden at other seasons. And maybe, just maybe, you will begin to add a few bulbs or a shrub or two that you can enjoy next winter. The new planting in turn may prompt you to add more the following year and every year after that. I hope there will be no stopping you. You will find new places to plant that you cannot even imagine now while walking around your garden. The best gardens are built that way; each planting opens the gardener's eye and imagination to a new place that could use a change. Each fall's plantings accelerate, picking up speed and heft like the snowball rolling down the hill, until the garden becomes a whirl of activity as bulbs, conifers, and shrubs are planted to ensure each winter's garden outshines the one before.

Then, of course, your neighbors and visitors will notice the difference, and they too will begin as you did to alter their winter landscape by tucking a few things in here and there. Before we know it, there will be an awakening in your neighborhood that will spread to your town, on to your state, and across our country. What a wonderful world that would be. If we are going to dream of influencing people and making changes, it makes no sense to make them small dreams.

If we are lucky, a little of my zeal and passion will light a flame under you. And you will be fired up to plant a garden that will keep the flame lit for a lifetime.

OPPOSITE: An arch of bent branches is lit with a string of lights as a contemporary twist on a holiday tradition.

Sources for Winter Plants

Trees, Shrubs, and Perennials

Forestfarm
990 Tetherow Road
Williams, OR 97544-9599
Phone: 541-846-7269
Web site: www.forestfarm.com
They have a wide selection of unusual trees and shrubs. Even though they ship small sizes, the plants are well worth the time watching them grow.

Holly Ridge Nursery
5925 South Ridge Road
Geneva, OH 44041
Phone: 800-465-5901
Nursery: 440-466-0134
Web site: cat.hollyridgeonline.com
The Web site is for information only, not for ordering.

Klehm Nursery
4210 North Duncan Road
Champaign, IL 61822
Phone: 800-553-3715
Fax: 217-373-8403
Web site: www.klehm.com
E-mail: klehm@soltec.net
Best known for peonies, this family company carries many shrubs, trees, and perennials for winter. The plants are packed and sent with great care. Their catalog is filled with wonderful information.

Mountain Maples
Japanese Maple Specialists
PO Box 220
Potter Valley, CA 95469
Phone: 888-707-6522

Web site: www.mountainmaples.com
E-mail: mtmaples@mountainmaples.com
They sell a wide assortment of Japanese maples that add interesting shapes to the landscape year-round.

White Flower Farm
PO Box 50, Route 63
Litchfield, CT 06759-0050
Phone: 800-503-9624
Web site: www.whiteflowerfarm.com
This catalog is filled with top-notch information. The plants are also packed with care.

Andre Viette Farm & Nursery
994 Long Meadow Road
Fishersville, VA 22939
Phone: 800-575-5538
Web site: www.viette.com
Web site: www.inthegardenradio.com
Andre Viette hosts a weekly Saturday morning call-in radio show. He knows his stuff and his catalog is filled with unusual plants.

The Primrose Path
921 Scottdale Dawson Road
Scottdale, PA 15683
Phone: 724-887-6756
Web site: www.theprimrosepath.com

Siskiyou Rare Plant Nursery
2115 Talent Avenue
Talent, OR 97540
Phone: 541-535-7103
Web site: www.srpn.net

Bulbs

Temple Nursery
PO Box 591
Trumansburg, NY 14886
They sell snowdrops "in the green." Write for a catalog as they do not accept phone orders and do not have an e-mail address.

Brent and Becky's Bulbs
7900 Daffodil Lane
Gloucester, VA 23061
Phone: 804-693-3966
Fax: 804-693-9436
Web site: www.brentandbeckysbulbs.com
They offer a wide selection of high quality bulbs. Every bulb is pictured in their catalog.

John Scheepers, Inc.
23 Tulip Drive
Bantam, CT 06750
Phone: 860-567-0838
Fax: 860-567-5323
Web site: www.johnscheepers.com
E-mail: catalog@johnscheepers.com
This is a very reliable company.

Van Engelen Inc.
23 Tulip Drive
PO Box 638
Bantam, CT 06750
Phone: 860-567-8734
Fax: 860-567-5323
Web site: www.vanengelen.com

McClure & Zimmerman
108 W. Winnebago Street
PO Box 368
Friesland, WI 53935-0368
Phone: 800-883-6998
Fax: 800-374-6120
Web site: www.mzbulb.com
Bulbs are packaged with planting instructions as well as notes on their size, color, and bloom time—very helpful.

Bibliography

Armitage, Allan M. *Herbaceous Perennial Plants*. Athens, GA: Varsity Press, 1989.

Bryan, John E. *Bulbs*. Rev. ed. Portland, OR: Timber Press, 2002.

Buchanan, Rita. *Taylor's Weekend Gardening Guides: The Winter Garden*. New York: Houghton Mifflin, 1997.

Callaway, Dorothy J. *The World of Magnolias*. Portland, OR: Timber Press, 1994.

Crockett, James Underwood. *Trees*. New York: Time-Life Books, 1972.

Dirr, Michael A. *Manual of Woody Landscape Plants*. 5th ed. Champaign, IL: Stipes Publishing Company, 1998.

Eck, Joe, and Wayne Winterrowd. *A Year at North Hill*. Toronto: Little, Brown and Company, 1995.

Harnden, Philip. *A Gardener's Guide to Frost*. Minocqua, WI: Willow Creek Press, 2003.

Hartlage, Richard W. "Small Wonders," *Horticulture* magazine, November 1997.

Hinkley, Daniel J. *Winter Ornamentals*. Seattle, WA: Sasquatch Books, 1993.

Jekyll, Gertrude. *Gertrude Jekyll's Colour Schemes for the Flower Garden*. London: Frances Lincoln, 1988.

Lawrence, Elizabeth. *Gardens in Winter*. Baton Rouge, LA: Claitor's, 1973.

Libbrecht, Kenneth. *The Snowflake: Winter's Secret Beauty*. Stillwater, MN: Voyageur Press, 2003.

———. *The Little Book of Snowflakes*. Stillwater, MN: Voyageur Press, 2004.

Loewer, Peter, and Larry Mellichamp. *The Winter Garden: Planning and Planting for the Southeast*. Mechanicsburg, PA: Stackpole Books, 1997.

Price, Eluned. *The Winter Garden*. New York: Smithmark, 1996.

Roehm, Carolyne. *Carolyne Roehm's Winter Notebook*. New York: HarperCollins, 1999.

Simeone, Vincent A. *Wonders of the Winter Landscape*. Batavia, IL: Ball Publishing, 2005.

Thomas, Graham Stuart. *Colour in the Winter Garden*. 3rd rev. London: J. M. Dent & Sons, 1984.

———. *Cuttings from My Garden Notebook*. Sagaponack, NY: Sagapress, 1997.

van Gelderen, D. M. *Conifers: The Illustrated Encyclopedia*. Vol. I and II. Portland, OR: Timber Press, 1996.

Vaucher, Hugues. *Tree Bark: A Color Guide*. Portland, OR: Timber Press, 2003.

Verey, Rosemary. *The Garden in Winter*. London: Frances Lincoln, 2006.

Acknowledgments

I am grateful to many people. Barbara Winkler, formerly the executive editor at *Family Circle*, helped me with the research and writing of this book. Elvin Mc Donald, deputy editor at *Better Homes and Gardens,* suggested many ideas, and we talked through each and every one. I have had the good fortune to work for both of them.

The team at Rodale, Margot Schupf and Nancy N. Bailey, couldn't be easier to work with. This book was Margot's idea and Nancy edited it, asking probing questions and polishing the final text. Their input and ideas were invaluable.

Doug Turshen designed the book and assisted on some of the photo shoots. He brought the book's ideas to life. Richard Felber was invaluable on many photo shoots. His experienced eye and expertise make his pictures remarkable. Richard also loaned me pictures from his personal collection. Richard Warren photographed many of the beautiful winter scenes and is always a delight to work with. My daughter Margaret and her husband, Richard Klemm, pinch hit, shooting photos for the book when a professional photographer wasn't available. Dr. Kenneth Libbrecht, Jim Large, and the Denver Botanic Garden also shared their photos.

Gina Norgard sorted through pictures and researched topics on the Internet as well helping me weekly in the garden. Jose Palacio has built our retaining walls, terraces, arbors, fences, garden furniture, and gazebos over many years. Carlos Valle, equipped with his sunny personality and quick wit, has helped maintain our garden.

Many gardeners shared their garden's stories, their wisdom, and their photos: Dr. Allan M. Armitage, Patricia Altschul, Anne Busquet, J. Barrry Ferguson, Conni Cross, Vincent A. Simeone and Peter Atkins of Planting Fields Arboretum, Jim and Carol Large, Kim Johnson and the staff at Old Westbury Gardens, Todd Forrest, curator of conifers at the New York Botanical Garden, Wayne Winterrowd and Joe Eck of North Hill Design, Tom Cooper, Ron Solt, Alan Branhagen, director of horticulture at Powell Gardens, Kay Macy, Les Brake, Dennis Schrader, Bill Smith, Mary Riley Smith, Tony Smith, and Deedee Wigmore.

Photo Credits

Photographs are by Suzy Bales except for the following:

Scott Dressel-Martin: 32–33, 78, 102, 147

Richard Felber: vii, 2, 7, 25, 38 *(left)*, 45, 66–67, 82–83, 115 *(bottom)*, 130, 149, 155, 157, 158, 166, 167, 169, 171 *(top left)*, 173, 178–179, 181, 183, 189, 191

John Granen: 141, 142–143, 145

Richard Klemm: xix, 20, 85

Dr. Kenneth Libbrecht: 107

Gina Norgard: 61

Tony Smith: 4–5

Richard Warren: i, 23, 27, 51, 53, 52, 69, 76, 77, 87, 95, 108–109, 124 *(left)*, 133, 152, 156, 160, 162–163, 170, 172, 174 *(left)*, 177, 185, 186–187

Index

Boldface page numbers indicate photographs or illustrations. Underscored references indicate boxed text, tables or charts.

A

Abies. *See also* Fir
    growing in containers, 134–35, **134**
Abies alba 'Green Spiral', 38
Abies balsamea 'Nana', 42
Abies concolor 'Compacta', 42
Abies fraseri, 40
Abies koreana
    'Aurea', 41
    'Silberlocke' (Silver Curls), 41, **41**, <u>48</u>
    'Starker's Dwarf', 42, **42**
Abies nordmanniana 'Golden Spreader', 40
Accessories, **82–83**, 139
    birdbaths, **124**, 180–81, **180, 181**
    containers (*see* Containers)
    window boxes, **135**, 138, **138**
Acer, **4–5**
Acer griseum, 27
Acer palmatum, 25, **25**
Acer palmatum 'Sango-Kaku', 27
Adonis (adonis), 99, **99**, <u>99</u>
Adonis amurensis, 99
Adonis vernalis, <u>99</u>
Allium, **148, 171, 182, 183**
Alnus incana (gray alder), 30
Arbors, **1, 4–5, 9**
Arborvitae, 42, <u>48</u>, **163**
Aronia arbutifolia 'Brilliantissima', 84
Arum italicum 'Pictum', 64
Astilbe, 104–5
Azalea, 52

B

Balsam, <u>37</u>
Bamboo, heavenly, 57–58, **57, 61,** <u>86</u>, **135**
Barberry, Japanese, 77, **78**, 79
Bark
    basics types of, <u>29</u>
    shrubs and trees with colorful, 26–27
    shrubs and trees with interesting, 26–27, **28**, <u>29</u>
Beauty berries, 79, <u>86</u>, **138**
Beech, **20–21**, 22
Begonias, strawberry, <u>92</u>
Berberis thunbergii, 77, **78**, 79
Berberis thunbergii atropurpurea (Japanese barberry), 79. *See also* Barberry, Japanese
Berries
    in Christmas and winter decorations, <u>86–87</u>, **136, 137, 138, 161, 163, 164, 165**
    shrubs with colorful, 54–58, **55, 56, 57, 59** (*see also* Holly)
    shrubs with interesting, 72, 76–87, **76, 77, 78, 80, 81,** <u>86–87</u>
Betula, 27. *See also* Birch
Betula lutea, 27
Betula nigra, 27, **27**
Betula pendula 'Youngii', 24
Bignonia capreolata, 8
Birch
    river, 27, **27**
    weeping European
        'Youngii', 24
    white, 27
    yellow, **20–21**, 27
Birdbaths, **124**, 180–81, **180, 181**
Birds, <u>84</u>, **85**
Bittersweet, <u>86</u>. *See also* Firethorn
Black-eyed Susan, seed heads of, 104
Bluebirds, **85**
Boxwood, **2, 15**
    common, 60, 148
    in Christmas decorations, **160, 171, 172,** <u>176</u>
    littleleaf, 138
Brake, Les, 140, 142–44, **142**
Bulbs
    basics of, <u>128</u>
    cost-effectiveness of, <u>116</u>
    dividing, 128
    fragrant, <u>6</u>, <u>112</u>
    growing in containers, **124**, 139, **139**, 180, **180**
    layering, <u>126</u>
    naturalizing, 126–27, **127**
    planting spring-flowering, 10
    spring-flowering as planting partners, 8, 10
    transplanting "in the green," 116, 128–29
Busquett, Anne
    garden of, **22–23**
Butterbur, 98–99
Buxus microphylla
    'Kingswood Dwarf', 138

Buxus sempervirens, 60, 148. *See also* Boxwood
    'Elegantissima', 60, 148
    'Latifolia Maculata', 60, 148
    'Marginata', 148

C

Calamagrostis × *acutiflora* 'Karl Foerster', 103
Callicarpa, 79
Callicarpa americana, <u>86</u>
Callicarpa bodinieri var. *giraldii* 'Profusion', 79
Callicarpa japonica 'Leucocarpa', 79
Camellia (camellia), **ix,** 74, **75**
Camellia japonica
    hardy cultivars, 74
Carex, 103
Carex flacca 'Blue Zinger', 103
Carex flagellifera 'Kiwi', 103
Carex siderostica 'Variegata', 103
Catalogs, <u>11</u>
Catalpa speciosa (catalpa), 30
Cedar, <u>48</u>, <u>176</u>
    dwarf western red cedar *(Thuja)*
        'Cuprea', 135
    golden Atlas *(Cedrus)*
        'Aurea', 37, 40
    'Silver Mist' *(Cedrus)*, 40–41
    weeping blue Atlas *(Cedrus)*, <u>48</u>, **49**
        'Glauca', 43, **43,** <u>48</u>
Cedrus atlantica
    'Aurea', 37
    'Glauca', 43, **43,** <u>48</u>
Cedrus deodara 'Silver Mist', 40–41
Cedrus libani 'Aurea', 40
Chamaecyparis, 37, 43, <u>48</u>
    with golden foliage, **35,** 39–40
Chamaecyparis lawsoniana, 43
    'Columnaris', 43
    'Ellwoodii', 37, 43, **138, 173**
    'Intertexta', 43
Chamaecyparis nootkatensis, 38
    'Pendula', **36,** 38, <u>48</u>
Chamaecyparis obtusa, 42
    'Bluefeathers', 41
    'Crippsii', 37, 39–40, **39**
    'Gold Drop', 42
    'Nana', 42
    'Nana Aurea', 40
    'Nana Gracilis', <u>48</u>
    'Pygmaea Aurescens', 44
    'Snowflake', 41
    'Spiralis', 42
Chamaecyparis pisifera
    'Compacta Variegata', **39**
    'Filifera Aurea', 40
    'Gold Mop' ('Mops', "Golden Mops'), 44
Checkerberry, 64

Cherry
    cornelian *(Cornus)*, 72
    weeping *(Prunus)*, 22, 24
        'Shidare Yoshino', 24
Chionodoxa, 10, 118
Chionodoxa forbesii, 118
Chionodoxa luciliae (C. gigantea), 118
Chokeberry, red, 84
Christmas decorations. *See also* Winter decorations
    arrangements, **156, 161,** <u>161</u>, **170,** 172–73, **172, 173, 185, 186, 187**
    berries for (*see* Berries)
    evergreens (*see* Evergreens)
    flowers in (*see* Flowers)
    fruits useful in (*see* Fruits)
    garlands, 166, **167, 182, 189**
    hanging cones, **87**
    kissing balls, 178–79, **187**
    Old Westbury Gardens techniques, <u>184</u>, **185,** <u>186–87</u>, **186, 187**
    package trims from the garden, 174, **174, 175**
    pinecones in, **165, 166, 173**
    scent of, <u>37</u>
    swags, **157,** 166, **166, 185**
    topiaries, **17, 167, 185**
    trees, **167, 171**
        decorating with dried flowers, 170
        living, <u>154</u>, **155**
        miniature handmade, 170, **171**
    wreaths, **152–53,** 156–66, **158, 159, 160, 161,** <u>162–63</u>, **162, 163, 164, 165,** 172, **172, 174, 184, 186**
Christmas rose, 90
Cimicifuga, seed heads of, 105
Coneflower, seed heads of, 104
Conifers, **32–33**. *See also* Evergreens; specific tree
    as living Christmas trees, <u>154</u>, **155**
    classifications of, <u>44</u>
    defined, 37
    dwarf, 42, **42,** <u>42</u>, <u>48</u>
    growing in containers, 134–35, **134,** 138, **138**
    in Christmas and winter decorations (*see* Evergreens)
    in winter landscape, **4–5**
    large trees, 43, **43**
    miniature, <u>48</u>, **173**
    New York Botanical Garden's Top Ten, <u>48</u>
    planting, <u>48</u>
    protecting in winter, <u>46</u>
    role of in winter garden, 37
    spreading, 44, **45,** 46
    unusual, 46–47
    weeping, 44
    with blue foliage, <u>40</u>, 41
    with golden foliage, 38–40, **38–39, 136**
    with silver foliage, 40–41, **41**

Containers, **130–31, 133, 134, 136, 137,** 146, **147, 148, 149**
  growing dwarf evergreens in, 134–35, **134, 148, 149**
  window boxes, **135,** 138, **138**
Coralberry, 84
Cornelian cherry, 72
Cornus alba, 10, 26. *See also* Dogwood
Cornus mas, 72
Corylopsis, 70–72, **70**
  'Winterthur', 71–72
Corylopsis pauciflora, 70–71
Corylopsis spicata, 71
Corylus avellana contorta, 22, 24
Cotoneaster (cotoneaster), 10, 58, **59**
Cotoneaster dammeri 'Streib's Findling', 58
Cotoneaster horizontalis, 10
Cotoneaster horizontalis var. *perpusillus,* 58
Cotoneaster 'Variegatus', 58
Cowslip, English, 96–97, **97**
Crab apples, 7, 22, 30–31, **31,** 40, 86
Cranberry bush, American, 81
Crape myrtle 'Natchez', **28**
Crocus (crocus), 10, 116–17, 116, **117, 129, 139**
  snow, 6, **110–11**
Crocus biflorus 'Miss Vain', 116–17
Crocus chrysanthus, 117
  'Advance', 117
  'Goldilocks', 117
Crocus imperati, 116
Crocus sieberi 'Tricolor', 116
Crocus tommasinianus, 117, **117**
  'Barr's Purple', 117
  'Ruby Giant', 117
Cross, Conni
  garden of, **35**
Cross vine, 8
Cupressus, 43. *See also* Cypress *(Cupressus)*
Cupressus 'Golden Wilma', 135
Cupressus macrocarpa 'Goldcrest', 148
Cupressus sempervirens, 148
Cyclamen (cyclamen), in Christmas decorations, **164**
Cyclamen coum (cyclamen), 122
Cypress *(Cupressus)*
  false *(see Chamaecyparis obtusa;* False cypress)
  Hinoki *(see Chamaecyparis obtusa;* False cypress)
  Italian, **134,** 148
  Lawson *(see Chamaecyparis lawsoniana;* False cypress)
  lemon, **134, 138**
    'Golden Wilma', 135
  light requirements of, 48
  Monterey
    'Goldcrest', 148
  Nootka *(see Chamaecyparis nootkatensis)*
  true, 43

D
Daffodils, 6, 8, 10, **13, 19, 95, 119,** 122–24, **123, 124, 125, 127**
Dahlias, drying, **108**
Daphne mezereum (February daphne), 10
Dash, Robert
  garden of, 14–15, **15**
Dewberry, 64
Dogwood
  red-twig, 10, 26, **130–31, 136,** 174, **174**
  yellow-twig, 26

E
Eranthis cilicica, 116. *See also* Winter aconite
Eranthis hyemalis, 116. *See also* Winter aconite
Erica, 94–95, **94**
Erica carnea, 94, **94**
Erica × *darleyensis,* 94
Eryngium giganteum, 40
Euonymus, in Christmas decorations, **164**
Euonymus fortunei (wintercreeper)
  'Gracilis', **62,** 63
  'Kewnsis', 63
  'Moonshadow', 63, 138
  'Sunspot', 63
  'Variegata', 63
Euonymus japonicus (euonymus)
  'Silver Princess', 148
Evergreen perennials, as groundcovers, 63–65
Evergreens. *See also* Conifers; specific tree or shrub
  as hedges, **82–83**
  broadleaf, 50–61, 50, **51, 52, 53, 54, 55, 56, 57, 59, 61**
  for Christmas and winter decorations, 135, **135, 136, 137, 152–53,** 154, **157, 158, 160, 161,** 163, **163, 164, 165, 166, 171,** 176, **177, 185**
  growing in containers, 134–35, **134, 148, 149**
Evergreen vines, as groundcovers, 62–63, **62, 65**

F
Fagus grandifolia, 22. *See also* Beech
Fagus sylvatica 'Pendula', 22
False cypress, 37, 39–40, 43, 44, 48. *See also Chamaecyparis*
  'Bluefeathers', 41
  'Crippsii', 37, 39–40
  Hinoki, 42
    'Gold Drop', 42
    'Nana', 42
    'Nana Gracilis, 48
    'Spiralis', 42

False cypress (*cont.*)
    Lawson
        'Columnaris', 43
        'Ellwoodii', 43, **138**
        'Ellwoodii', 37
        'Intertexta', 43
        'Nana Aurea', 40
        'Nana Filifera', 40
        'Pygmaea Aurescens', 44
        'Snowflake', 41
Fences, **1, 4–5**
Ferns, **175**
Festuca glauca (fescue), 103
Fetterbush. *See Leucothoe*
Filbert. *See Corylus avellana contorta*
Fir. *See also Abies*
    balsam
        'Nana', 42
    Frasier, 40
    growing dwarf in containers, 134–35, **134**
    in Christmas decorations, **152–53, 157, 163,**
        165, 176, **186**
    Korean
        'Aurea', 41
        'Silberlocke' (Silver Curls), 41, **41,** 48
        'Starker's Dwarf', 42, **42**
    white
        'Compacta', 42
    with golden foliage, 40
    'Golden Spreader', 40
Firethorn, 54, **55,** 86
Flowers
    dried, 108–9, **108, 109**
        in Christmas decorations, 156, **158,** 159,
            159, 164, 165, 170, **171,** 182, **182, 183**
        Kay Macy's drying method, 108–9
    fresh
        in Christmas decorations, **161, 164, 185**
    shrubs with interesting winter, 68–75, **69, 70,**
        71, 73, 75
    trees with interesting winter, 28, 30
    with attractive seedheads, 104–5
Forget-me-nots, **39, 97**
Forsythia, 8
Fountain grass, 103
Fragrance
    in winter garden, 6
    of winter-flowering bulbs, 112
    scent of Christmas, 37
    shrubs for, 68, 72
Frost, 18–19
Fruits
    trees with decorative, 30–31, 30
    useful in arrangements, 86, **161**

G

Galanthus, 114–16, 114, **115, 117.** *See also*
    Snowdrops

Galanthus elwesii, 114, 116
Galanthus nivalis, 114–15, **115**
Garden design, 14–15, 34. *See also* Accessories;
        Arbors; Fences; Hedges; Walls
    analysis of existing plan, 2
    do's and don'ts, 12
    ornaments in, 16, **16**
    structural elements in
        deciduous trees for, 24
        living, **2**
        man-made, **1, 2,** 3, **4–5**
        plants as, **1,** 6–7
    topiary in, **17, 149**
Gaultheria procumbens, 64
    'Wintergreen', 138
Ginkgo, **15,** 31
Glory-of-the-snow, 10, 118, **123**
Golden rain tree, 30
Gomphrena, **171**
Grape hyacinths, 118, 120
Grasses, ornamental, 100–104, **100, 101, 102**
Groundcovers, 62–65, **62, 65**
    as planting partners, 10
    conifers as, 44, **45,** 46
    Cotoneaster as, 58, **59**
    evergreen and spring-flowering bulbs as, 10
Grouseberry, 64

H

Hakonechloa, 'Aureola', **100**
Hamamelis, 68–70, **69**
Hamamelis × *intermedia*, 8, 70, **71**
Harry Lauder's walking stick, 22, 24
Hazelnut. *See Corylus avellana contorta*
Heath, 94–95, **94**
Heather, **95**
Heavenly bamboo, 57–58, **57, 61,** 86, **135**
Hedera helix. See also Ivy
    English, 63
        'Buttercup', 63
        'Glacier', 63
        'Goldheart', **9,** 63, **65**
Hedges, **2,** 6–7, 6, **7, 82–83**
Helictotrichon sempervirens, 103
Helleborus (Hellebore), **13,** 90–94, **91, 93, 98, 125**
Helleborus argutifolius (Corsican hellebore), 92
Helleborus foetidus (bear's foot hellebore), **xi,** 92
Helleborus × *hybridus* (hellebore), 90, **91, 93**
    'Heronswood Doubles', 92
    'Heronswood Red', 92
Helleborus niger (Christmas rose), 90
Helleborus orientalis (Lenten rose), 92
Hemlock, 44, 47, 48. *See also Tsuga*
Hen and chicks, 64
Holly, 50–52, 50, **51, 52, 53,** 86. *See also Ilex*
    American, 50–51, **51,** 52, **52, 53,** 77, 86
    deciduous (winterberry), **53, 66–67,** 76–77, 86

'Aurantiaca', **53, 76, 77, 163**
'Jim Dandy', 52
'Sundrops', 76–77
'Winter Red', **53, 77**
English, 51, **53**
in Christmas and winter decorations, **87, 134,**
135, 136, 137, 152–53, **161, 164, 165,**
166, 176, **187**
Japanese, 148
legends about, 50
longstalk, 77
sex life of, 52
Holly grapes *(Mahonia)*, 72, **73**
Honesty, silver pods of, 105
Honeysuckle vines, **178–79**
Hosta, 105
Hydrangea
climbing, 8, **9**
dried, **88–89,** 105, **165, 171**

I

Ice in Fire, **xix,** 140–45, **141, 142, 143, 144,** 144,
145
Ilex, 50–52, 50, **51, 52, 53,** 86
'Honey Maid', **53**
legends about, 50
sex life of, 52
Ilex aquifolium
'Alba-marginata', **53**
'Winter Queen', **53**
Ilex crenata
'Sky Pencil', 148
Ilex opaca, 50–51, 86
'Christmas Snow', 77
'Jersey Prince', 52
'Lake City', 50
'Morgan's Gold', 77
'Ms. Courtney', **51**
'Satyr Hill', 50–51
Ilex pedunculosa, 72, 77
Ilex verticillata, 76–77, 86
'Aurantiaca', **53, 76, 77, 163**
'Sundrops', 76–77
'Winter Red', **53, 77**
Iris (iris)
dwarf (rock garden), **110–11,** 120–21, **121**
Iris bucharica, 121
Iris danfordiae, 121
Iris reticulata, **120,** 121
Iris unguicularis (winter iris, Algerian iris),
121
Ironwood, Persian, 27
Ivy, 8
as container plant, **136**
English, **9,** 63, **65**
in Christmas and winter decorations, **87, 136,**
171, 174, **175,** 176, **185**

J

Jasminum nudiflorum (winter jasmine), 8, 73
Juniperus (juniper), 86
in Christmas and winter decorations, **136, 137,**
158, 176, **187**
Juniperus chinensis, **38**
'Torulosa', **148**
Juniperus conferta (shore juniper), 44, 46
'Blue Lagoon', 46
'Silver Mist', 41, 46
'Sunsplash', 46
Juniperus horizontalis (rug juniper), **35,** 44,
45
'Bar Harbor', 44
'Blue Chip', 44
'Emerald Spreader', 44
'Heidi', 44
'Lime Glow', 44, 48
'Mother Lode', 44
'Prince of Wales', 44
'Wiltonii', 44
Juniperus squamata
'Blue Star', 41, **138**

K

Kale, **134**
Kalmia, 60
Kalmia latifolia 'Carol', 60
Kalmia myrtifolia, 60
'Olympic Wedding', 60
Koelreuteria paniculata, 30

L

Lagerstroemia 'Natchez', **28**
Larch, light requirements of, 48
Lavender, in Christmas decorations, **164,**
175
Lenten rose, 92
Leucothoe, 58, 60
Leucothoe axillaris, **61**
Leucothoe fontanesiana, 10
as Christmas decoration, 176
'Rainbow', 10, 58, 60
'Scarletta', 60, **61**
Lily-of-the-valley shrub, 54, **54**
Lilyturf, 63, 105
Linden, **22–23**
Liquidambar styraciflua, 30
Liriope, 63, 105
Liriope majestic 'Majestic', 63
Liriope muscari 'Pee Dee Gold Ingot',
63
London plane tree, growth rate of, 31
Lunaria annua, 105
Lungwort, 97, **97**

M

Macy, Kay, 108–9, **108**
Magnolia (magnolia)
  in Christmas decorations, **163, 165, 172,** <u>176,</u>
    185
Magnolia grandiflora (Southern magnolia), 25
Magnolia stellata (star magnolia), 10, 25
Mahonia aquifolium, 72, **73**
Mahonia japonica, 72
Mahonia × *media*, 72
Malus, 30–31, <u>86</u>
  'Christmas Holly', 31
  'Donald Wyman', 30–31
  'Red Jade', 31
  'Sugartyme', 31, **31**
  'Winter Gold', 31
Malus sargentii, 30–31
Maple
  coral bark, **4–5**
    'Sango-Kahu', 27
  Japanese, 25, **25**
  paperbark, 27
Mexican feather grass, in arrangements, **134**
Miscanthus, **134**
Miscanthus sinensis, **101, 102**
  'Variegatus', 100, 103
Mountain laurel, 60
  'Carol', 60
  'Olympic Wedding', 60
Muscari, 118, 120
Muscari armeniacum 'Christmas Pearl', 120
Muscari azureum, 120
Myrtle, 63

N

Nandina domestica, 57–58, **57,** <u>86</u>
  'Harbor Dwarf', 57–58
  'Wood's Dwarf', 58, **61, 135**
Narcissus, 122–24, **123, 124.** *See also* Daffodils
  'February Gold', 122, 124, **124**
  'Jenny', 124
  'Peeping Tom', 124
  'Tete-a-tete', 124, **124**
  'Trevithain', 124
Narcissus asturiensis, 122
Narcissus bulbocodium conspicuous, 124
  'Golden Bells', 124

O

Oat grass, blue, 103
Osmanthus heterophyllus, 60
  'Goshiki', **53,** 60, **61**
  'Purpureus', 60
  'Variegatus', 60

P

Pachysandra (pachysandra), 63
  'Silver Edge', 63
Pachysandra procumbens, 63
Panicum virgatum 'Heavy Metal', 103
Paperwhites, **172**
Parrotia persica, 27
Pennisetum alopercuroides, 103
Perennials, with silver foliage, 40
Perilla, invasiveness of, 104
Petasites, **98**
Petasites hybridus, 98–99
Petasites japonicus, 98–99
Phalaris arundinacea, 103
  'Strawberries and Cream', 103
Pheasant's eye, 99, **99,** <u>99</u>
Picea, 43
Picea abies 'Pendula', 44
Picea glauca 'Conica', 135
Picea orientalis, 43
  'Skyland', 37, **38,** 39
Picea pungens
  'Bakeri', 135
  'Hoopsi', 41
  'Iseli Fastigite', 43
  'Koster', 41
  'Moerheim', 41
  'R. H. Montgomery', <u>48</u>
Pieris japonica, 54, **54**
  'Daisen', 54
  'Flamingo', 54
  in Christmas decorations, **152–53,** <u>176</u>
  'Valley Valentine', 54
  'White Cascade', 54
Pigeonberry, 64
Pinus (pine)
  cones of in Christmas decorations, **165, 166,**
    173
  in Christmas and winter decorations, **134, 152–**
    53, 163, 166, <u>176</u>
  Japanese umbrella (*see Sciadopitys verticillata*)
  light requirements of, <u>48</u>
  with golden foliage, 40
Pinus bungeana (lacebark pine), 46
Pinus cembra
  'Nana', 135
Pinus densiflora
  'Oculus-draconis' (dragon's eye pine), 46
Pinus mugo
  'Ophir', 40
  'Winter Gold', 40
Pinus strobus (white pine)
  'Blue Mist' (dwarf white), 41
  'Sea Urchin' (miniature eastern white pine), <u>48</u>
Pinus sylvestris
  'Aurea', 40

'Gold Coin', 40
'Gold Metal', 40
Pinus thunbergii (Japanese black pine), 46
Pinus wallichiana
    'Umbraculifera', 46
    'Zebrina' (variegated Himalayan pine), 48
Plum yew, light requirements of, 48
Pollarding, 26–27
Primula (primroses), 96–97, **96, 97, 127**
Primula polyanthus, 96, **97**
Primula tomasinii
    'Penumbra', 96
    'You and Me', 96
Primula veris (English cowslip), 96–97, **97**
Pruning, 14
Prunus yedoensis, 24
    'Shidare Yoshino', 24
Pulmonaria, 97, **97**
Pulmonaria angustifolia 'Azurea', 97
Pulmonaria officinalis 'Sissinghurst White', 97
Pulmonaria saccharata 'Mrs. Moon', 97, **97**
Puschkinia scilloides (puschkinia), 118
Pyracantha, 54, 55, 86
    'Fiery Cascade', 54
    'Teton', 54

R

Red bud, **13**
Rhododendron, **136, 137**
Rhododendron yakushimanum, 52, **52**
    'Mist Maiden', 52
Ribbon grass, 'Strawberries & Cream', 103
Rock gardens, **32–33**
Rosa multiflora, 86
Rose hips
    in Christmas and winter decorations, 86, **87,**
        135, 136, 137, 160, 164, 165, 171, 174,
        175, 187
Roses, 8, 81, **171**
Roxberry, 64

S

Salix, rooting from twigs, 28
Salix alba ssp. *vitellina*
    'Britzensis', 26
    'Hutchinson's Yellow', 26
Salix × *chaenomeloides*, 28, 30
    'White Kittens', 30
Salix discolor, 8
Salix gracilistyla 'Melanostachys', 28
Salix hookeriana, 28
Salix matsudana, 24
    'Golden Curls', 24
    'Koidzumi', **147**
    'Scarlet Curls', 24

Salix myrsinifolia
    'Nigricans', 26
Salvia, **171**
Saxifraga stolonifera, 92
Sciadopitys verticillata, 46–47, **47**
    'Anne Hadow', 46
    'Jim Cross', 47
    'Wintergreen', 46, 48
Scilla (scilla, squill, wood squill), 8, 10, **127**
Scilla siberica (scilla, squill, wood squill), 118, **119**
    'Spring Beauty', 118
Scilla tubergeniana (scilla, squill, wood squill), 118
Sea holly, 40
Sedge, 103
Sedum 'Autumn Joy', 104
Sedum rupestre 'Angelina', 64
Sedum spurium, 64
Seedheads
    of flowers, 104–5, **105**
    of ornamental grasses, 100–104, **100, 101, 102**
Sempervivum tectorum, 64
    'Royal Rudy', 64
Shrubs
    as garden framework, 7
    deciduous in winter landscape, **4–5**
    planting, 12, 70
    unusual, 84
    winter-flowering, 68–75, **69, 70, 71, 73, 75**
    with colorful fruits and berris, 54–58, **55, 56,**
        57, 59 (*see also* Holly)
    with interesting bark, 26–27, **28,** 29
    with interesting fruits and berries, 76–87, **76,**
        77, 78, 80, 81, 86–87
Silver dollar plant, 105
Silver grass. *See also Miscanthus*
    Japanese variegated, 100, 103
Skimmia japonica, 56, **56**
Skimmia reevesiana, 56, **56**
Smith, Tony and Mary
    garden of, **4–5**
Snowberry, 84
Snowdrops, **xvii,** 6, 10, **117, 129, 180**
    common, 114–15, 114, **115**
    giant, 114, 116
Snowflakes, **13,** 106–7, **107**
Solt, Ron, **162**
Spiketail, 74
Spruce, 43
    blue, **35, 87, 137, 166**
    Colorado blue, 41, 43, 135
    dwarf Alberta, 135, **138**
    dwarf blue Colorado, 48
    dwarf weeping, 44
    Oriental, 43
        'Skyland', 37, **38,** 39, **135, 152–53**
Spurge, Allegheny Mountain, 63
St. John's wort, 105

Stachyurus praecox, 74
Sunflowers, seed heads of, 105
Sweet gum, 30
Switch grass, 'Heavy Metal', 103
Symphoricarpos, 84
Symphoricarpos × doorenbosii, 84

T

Taxus baccata, 47, **48**, 148
Thuja, 42
Thuja 'Green Giant', <u>48</u>
Thuja occidentalis 'Teddy', 42
Thuja orientalis 'Rosedalis', 42
Thuja plicata 'Cuprea', 135
Thymus (thyme), 64
Thymus pseudolanuginosus (wooly thyme), 64
Thymus vulgaris 'Silver Edge', 64
Topiary, **17**, 148, **149, 167, 185**
Transplanting, "in the green', 116, 128–29
Trees. *See also* Conifers; Evergreens
    as structural element in garden design, 7
    deciduous
        with colorful bark, 26–27
        with interesting bark, 27, <u>29</u>
        with sculptural shapes, <u>24</u>
    planting, <u>12</u>
    with decorative winter fruit, 30–31, <u>30</u>
    with interesting winter flowers, 28, 30
Tsuga, 44, <u>48</u>
Tsuga canadensis 'Pendula', 47
Tulipa (tulip), 10, **13**, 108–9, 125
Tulipa clusiana (peppermint stick tulip), 125
Tulipa humilis alba coerulea oculata, 125
Tulipa humilis violacea (red crocus tulip), 125
Tulipa tarda, 125
Tulipa turkestanica, 125

U

USDA zones, jumping, <u>92</u>

V

Veronica longifolia, seedheads of, 104
Viburnum (viburnum), 80–81, **80, 81,** 84, **164**
Viburnum × bodnantense 'Dawn', **80,** 84
Viburnum dilatatum (linden viburnum), 81, 84

Viburnum trilobum (American cranberry bush), 81
Vinca minor, 63
    'Alba Aureavariegata', 63
    'Sterling Silver', 63
Vines, 8, **9, 62,** 63–64

W

Walls
    hedges as, 6–7, <u>6</u>
    stone, **2**
Wheat, in Christmas wreaths, **165**
Willow. *See also Salix*
    branches of as Christmas decoration, **156**
    coral embers, 26
    corkscrew, **147**
    curly, 24
    pussy, 8
    rooting from twigs, 28
    white pussy, 28, 30
Window boxes, **135**, 138, **138**
Winter aconite, <u>6,</u> **110–11,** 113, 116
Winterberry, 76–77, <u>86</u>. *See also* Holly
Wintercreeper, **62,** 63, 138
Winter decorations. *See also* Christmas decorations
    arrangements, **130–31, 133, 134, 135, 136, 137, 139, 146, 147**
    potted plants as, 134–35, **134, 136, 138, 139,** 148, **148, 149,** 150, **151**
    topiaries, **17,** 148, **148, 149**
Winter hazel, <u>6,</u> 70–72, **70, 71**
    spike (spike witch hazel), 71
Winter jasmine, 8, 73
Wisteria, **4–5,** 105
Witch hazel, 8, 68–70, **69, 71**
    spike *(Corylopsis spicata),* 71
Wreaths, **152–53,** 156–66, **158, 159, 160, 161, 162–63,** <u>162–63,</u> **163, 164, 165,** 172, **172, 174, 184, 186**
    using wreath forms, 159–60, **162,** <u>162–63,</u> **163**

Y

Yarrow, **165**
Yew, <u>48</u>
    English, 47, 148
Yucca, golden, **4–5**